SAY IT LOUD!
The Story of Rap Music

D1318452

THE STORY of Rap MUSIC

WITHDRAWN

SAY IT LOUD!

782.421
J77

by K. Maurice Jones

THE MILLBROOK PRESS
BROOKFIELD, CONNECTICUT

LIBRARY
MILWAUKEE AREA TECHNICAL COLLEGE
Milwaukee Campus

**FOR JADA, SHAMEL,
HARRY, GIBRAN,
JULIAN, MICHAELA,
AND KENNY CHIBOMBA**

Photographs in insert following page 32 courtesy of the National Museum of American Art, Washington, D.C./Art Resource, N.Y.: p. 1; The Bettmann Archive: pp. 2 (top), 5 (top); © The Phillips Collection, Washington, D.C.: p. 2 (bottom); the Collection of Archie Motley and Valerie Gerrard Browne, photo courtesy of the Chicago Historical Society: p. 3; Schomburg Center for Research in Black Culture, New York Public Library: pp. 4, 6; The Whitney Museum of American Art: p. 5 (bottom); AP/Wide World Photos: p. 7 (top); © Catherine Baulknight/Retna: p. 7 (bottom left); © 1993 Stephen Stickler: p. 7 (bottom right); The Museum of the National Center of Afro-American Artists, Boston: p. 8.

Photographs in insert following page 64 courtesy of © Ricky Powell: pp. 1, 2 (left), 3 (left); © Gregory Jackson: p. 2 (right); Alice Arnold: pp. 3 (middle), 5 (both), 6 (top right and bottom), 7 (top) left); AP/Wide World Photos: p. 3 (right); BJ Papas: pp. 4, 6 (top left); Jive Records: p. 7 (top right); Hollywood Records, photo by Sue Kwon: p. 7 (bottom); K. Maurice Jones: p. 8.

Library of Congress Cataloging-in-Publication Data
Jones, K. Maurice.
Say it loud! : the story of rap music / K. Maurice Jones.
p.   cm.
Includes bibliographical references and index.
Discography: p.
Summary: Explores the origins and development of rap music.
ISBN 1-56294-386-3   (lib. bdg.) ISBN 1-56294-724-9 (pbk.)
1. Rap (Music)—History and criticism—Juvenile literature.
ML3531.J66   1994
782.42164—dc20   93-1939   CIP   AC MN

Published by The Millbrook Press
2 Old New Milford Road, Brookfield, Connecticut 06804

Copyright © 1994 by K. Maurice Jones
All rights reserved
Printed in the United States of America
5   4   3

Contents

7 Prologue: Young Lions of America

Chapter One
15 The Roots of Rap

Chapter Two
25 Get On Up: The Rise of African-American Culture

Chapter Three
43 Back in the Day

Chapter Four
53 The Message Spreads

Chapter Five
79 Roots, Culture, Free Speech, and Technology

Chapter Six
95 Stylin' and Profilin'

Chapter Seven
105 Global Rap: Hip-Hop Rules

113 Epilogue: Young Lions Return

114 Notes
119 A Glossary of Hip-Hop Terms
121 Discography
123 Further Reading
125 Index

Yo, I'm chill, sit back and max,
telling ya'll about *Say It Loud*,
the story of the culture called rap.

You know I'm rippin' it, I'm dippin' kid.
I'm from the eastern side of Oakland,
smoking men, I don't be joking
and neither is my man on the side,
'cause he's right on the money
doing hip-hop service.
You nervous 'cause it's coming
and you cannot do anything about it.
My clout gets bigger and bigger by the day,
So, hey, ha-ha, just sit back
and chill, relax
and listen to The Story of Rap

TAJAI, SOULS OF MISCHIEF
"FREESTYLE FOR KEN JONES"

(RECITED IN VERNON'S JAMAICAN JERK PARADISE,
NEW YORK CITY, APRIL 23, 1993)

Prologue

YOUNG LIONS OF AMERICA

Yo man, give me that microphone and sit down,
'cause a brother like me is known to get down.
So get up on the rhyme,
'cause you'll find it's designed
to give sight to the blind
and enlighten the mind.

DEF JEF
"DROPPIN' RHYMES ON DRUMS"[1]

New
York
City.
Word was out about the Hieroglyphics posse from Oakland, California. Hieroglyphics, a group of rap acts brought together by Del Tha Funkee Homosapien, cousin of rapper Ice Cube, was about to introduce two new acts—Casual and Souls of Mischief—that were wicked. Street buzz had it that this crew from Oakland's East Bay neighborhood could sling rhymes so intricate that the dazed, unsuspecting listener would have to hit the rewind button—just to comprehend all the young brothers' syntax and concepts. "It's the slam, it's the straight beat," Del told everyone lucky enough to get an advance cassette of Casual and the Souls that was being played in clubs across the country. He declared: "You got to peep it [check it out]."[2]

That hype alone was enough to pack Mt. Fugi's Tropicanna Bar in New York City on a rainy spring night wall-to-wall. "Yeah man, this looks like a real hip-hop nation," a South African journalist, Mondli Makhanya, commented to an African-American colleague as he surveyed the crowd before him. Asians, whites, and blacks all packed the dance floor. "Unity in the house," a young woman on the dance floor shouted to no one in particular.

Track after track boomed: Run-D.M.C., L.L. Cool J, Ice Cube, Digable Planets—the finest in hip-hop. "Man, this is like being at a club in Soweto," the South African observed from the sidelines. "These homies up here ain't about no artificial flavor," an eavesdropping waitress informed him. "Welcome to America. This is as real as it gets."

Gradually the recorded music faded. "Yo, New York. Ya'll ready for some live sh——t, from Oakland?" Casual asked as he walked onto the club's small stage. "I'm gonna warm it up a little bit for the Souls of Mischief." He nodded to his audio man, who pushed a play button on the huge console near the stage. A new beat boomed from the speakers of the club's sound system. It was slow and funky. The crowd smiled, and nodded their heads to Casual's beat. Then he ripped a rhyme on the mike:

You done let me down.
I thought you would be dope,
but instead your sh——t's dead.
You get fed to alligators lurking in the moat.
Peep what I wrote,
you bit so hard I thought the sh——t was a quote.
But still I'm taxing, asking for competition
and any wack men, I stomp and dis 'em and easily.
And you can feel the pressure push when I bust,
and MCs will be trampling each other
trying to exit when I flex it.
The way I wreck sh——t is not unexpected.
I chose the best crews of MCs
and turn them into refugees.
I slaughter a lot of MCs
with all the styles I compile
and cut them off like vowels.[3]

Casual, a lighthouse of a man, smiled to the crowd as he rapped. The crowd roared back in approval.
"That's it ya'll, I'm outta here," a victorious Casual declared, as he concluded his set. "Hieroglyphics is in the house."

Casual passed his mike over to Opio, the tall, baby-faced dread-locked member of Souls of Mischief, as if he were presenting a baton to a teammate in a relay race. Without missing a beat, the deejay mixed in a harder, more uptempo bass-dominated beat.

Opio strutted out onstage with his partners Tajai, an earnest, clean-cut brother in the mode of a bow tie–wearing youth in the Nation of Islam; Phesto, a low key, slightly bookwormish-looking brother in a track suit; and A-Plus, resplendent in dreadlocks, nose ring, and baseball cap.

The crowd was pumped. The Souls began to rap—trading off verses and rhymes with the swiftness of basketball players making no-look passes on fast breaks. Tajai kicked it off:

> I find it fun to smash MCs into fine bits.
> I'm gonna get my just desserts for all
> the kids I must've hurt maybe.
> I trust that courtesy when dealing with
> folks is too much for the asking.
> Cool, I got the skill-crafted tools, massive fools,
> At my workbench and I'm wrenching mics from their graspin'.
> That's how it has been:
> The drills this I kill swift, I feel
> I'd better slay ya.

The crowd chanted Tajai's name. He raised his fist in the air, and Phesto drove up to center stage and reverse-slamdunked a rhyme:

> I proliferate a quicker fate to vigorous,
> Figure I kick concise puns twice that dissed,

Nifty detachin' a bath, latchin's to match.
My cataclysm, I give him a schism.
A stroke to croak him, I broke him,
Chokin' him by my syntax as I bend by impacts.

Phesto turned the spotlight over to A-Plus:

Yo, I'm willin' to bet, you willin' to sweat.
But end it will get you bruised.
I can't always step through crews
and abuse two's and three's.
Who's the Gees that know
me and hero; I know I'm fly bro'.
Now I'm gonna show you how the west coast smacks kids.
Yo, I'm rhyming swell, so the hell with a whack dis,
Generalizing, dissing before you ever see this!

Finally Opio stepped up for his solo:

Never matched the miraculous tactics.
I'll leave 'em broken, dumb, deaf.
I'm causing cardiac arrest; you need some rest.
Check as I'm chiseling riddles in your memory.
I wake up words, I excite rhymes.[4]

"Man, there's a saying we have back home," the totally enrap-
tured South African yelled in his friend's ear as the Souls continued to
"tear up" the club with their round-robin, funky expressions.

"What's that?" his partner yelled back.

"These guys are 'happy as Soweto boys in Soweto.' " The meaning was clear. The quartet of rappers might have been thousands of miles from the Union of South Africa, but they were clearly in control — or as the saying goes in hip-hop, "in the house."

Later, as they exited the club, the friends resumed their conversation. "There was something about the vibe in the club and those guys that reminded me of home," Mondli Makchanya said. "It was amazing. The setting was different, but the culture was the same. Those dudes are young lions of America."

Chapter ONE

The Roots of RAP

Rap is the most important

Rap is the most important popular music to emerge in America during the 1980s and 1990s. Yet rap is more than music or entertainment. The words rhythmically recited, chanted, or sung over music by the likes of Public Enemy, Queen Latifah, and Arrested Development represent a new sense of identity and belonging for young people in America — and throughout the world. Rap is the voice of a population that has been ignored by mainstream leaders and institutions. It is a culture.

The creation of young African Americans, rap reaches far beyond America's inner cities. Its booming bass and many voices resound on every continent. The sentiments expressed in many rap songs can't be dismissed as kid stuff. Politicians, clergy, journalists, and social scientists all ponder the utterances of rappers. Rap represents the pulse — thoughts, values, and experiences — of youth worldwide.

Perhaps rap is so profound because while it is new it also belongs to a centuries-old legacy of using language creatively in everyday life. Rap is part of the African-American oral and musical traditions that encompass the hidden messages of slave folktales; the call and response of the black church; the joy and pain of the blues; the jive talk and slang of disc jockeys, hipsters, and jazz musicians; the boasting of street talk; the sidesplitting wit of comedians; and the eloquence of black activists. Rap shares with them a common place of origin — West Africa.

THE MOTHERLAND The black ancestors of today's rappers, like the ancestors of most African Americans, came to the Americas during the North

Atlantic slave trade, which took place from the seventeenth to the nineteenth century. Before being sold into captivity, most of these Africans lived in the kingdoms of the Ashanti, the Ibo, Niger, and Benin. Today these regions are known as Senegal, Gambia, Liberia, the Ivory Coast, Ghana, Guinea, and Nigeria. Others came from present-day Angola, which is in southern Africa, or central Africa.

The oral tradition reigned supreme in these kingdoms. What the written word has been to Western culture, the spoken word was to these and other African cultures. In fact, until the twentieth century, most Africans generally conducted business, entered into treaties, and passed on history orally. And what a varied tradition it must have been. Today more than a thousand languages are spoken across the African continent. Probably even more tribal tongues were spoken in earlier centuries.

In traditional African societies, oration (speaking) was a sophisticated and highly developed form of expression. Depending on the occasion, oration could include reciting poetry, storytelling, and speaking to drumming and other musical accompaniment. Rarely was the word spoken plain, flat, and unembellished. Oration always served a dual purpose: to inform and to entertain.

The task of carrying out oration fell to the *griot*. Griots, the majority of them male, were professional singers and poets who traveled from region to region throughout their kingdoms carrying news of wars, births, deaths, and other events. The griot was an exalted person; his status was distinct from that of rulers, elders, medicine men, and others in African societies.

Being a griot was a demanding occupation. Since there was little emphasis on written language, the job required a remarkable memory and a love of details. The griot wore many hats. He was a historian, storyteller, comedian, reporter, mediator, social commentator, and often performer of religious ceremonies and rites of passage. Furthermore, the griot had to possess musical abilities. Griots often accompanied themselves on a harplike instrument called a *kora*.

Of the griot's training and status, musicologist Wolfgang Bender noted:

> All have in common an education in their own families from early childhood on. They learn to memorize texts and recitation. . . . The genealogy [family histories] of the ruling houses, the history of their dominions, great battles, conquests, and so on, are among the subjects of this oral transmission. The griots are rightly referred to as the archives and libraries of this part of Africa. Thus the famous proverb, 'whenever a griot dies, a library dies.' They were interpreters of current politics, transmitting messages and orders from the governing power to the people. As musicians with contacts with musicians outside the court, they were able to learn the opinion of common people and could convey sentiments of the populace to the ruler.[1]

Like the griot, even the lay person in traditional African society also had to have a command of language. This was mandatory in order to gain the respect of one's tribe and clan. Mastery of oral communication became, therefore, in Bender's words, "a practiced art, a challenge, a competitive sport, and a hobby."[2] When one understands the griot tradition in African societies, it is easy to understand how rappers like Chuck D, Ice-T, and Naughty by Nature can be self-appointed spokespersons for African-American youth.

THE MIDDLE PASSAGE In addition to the griot tradition, rap is rooted in the pain of black-American experience, which began with slavery. As Europeans conquered, settled, and, to many, stole the Americas, they required cheap labor to help build up their colonies and exploit natural resources for trade. Native Americans initially welcomed the whites to their continent. However, these people did not take kindly to the Europeans' intentions to put them to work as slaves in their own land. White settlers often responded to the natives' defiance by killing them. The Indians also succumbed to the strange diseases of the Europeans, such as smallpox. Others were pushed out of their homelands.

The settlers needed labor. They were building a new world and that required backbreaking work. Enter the Africans.

Slavery existed in African societies prior to the seventeenth century. But it was very different from the kind of bondage that characterized the North Atlantic slave trade. Slaves were taken in conquests or as repayment for debts or wrongs committed. The slaves were fully integrated into their new villages and tribes and granted many rights and privileges.

By all accounts, the North Atlantic slave trade was the largest and most traumatic forced movement of human beings in history. During the more than 150 years it operated, at least 10 million Africans were captured and shipped to the Americas on a hellish trans-Atlantic journey that became known as the Middle Passage.

The Middle Passage lasted from two months to a year, depending on the African port of departure and conditions on the open sea. Shackled and crammed into the lightless, airless holds of ships, Africans in Middle Passage descended into degradation and humiliation. Many committed suicide, jumping overboard into the Atlantic

Ocean rather than meet the unknown fate that awaited them at their journey's end. Others died of diseases. Those who survived were sold as slaves in the Americas.

BREAKING BONDAGE One of the biggest myths about slavery is that slave dealers and owners destroyed the spirit of their African captives. This proved to be too monumental a task. From the start of captivity in Africa, white slave dealers initiated a strict program of control and domination over their captives. It began with speech. Before the Africans descended into the filthy holds of the slave ships, they were separated from other members of their families and tribes.

The logic of the dealers was cold and precise. Mixing people from different regions, and thereby splitting up those who spoke the same language, would lessen the likelihood of an uprising at sea. Perhaps the oppressors understood all too well the power, and subsequent dangers, of the spoken word among their cargo.

Slave owners in the United States continued the same divide-and-silence philosophy once they purchased their human property. The whites held anything African in utter contempt. The Africans were forbidden from speaking in their native tongues. They were stripped of their real names and forced to assume names given to them by their masters (including their masters' surnames). Assuming a slave owner's name further separated a slave from his or her true identity and cultural roots.

The masters went even one step further in their process of bondage. They referred to the Africans generically as Negroes or niggers. Tribal and regional identifications such as Mandingo, Yoruba, or Mandinka, which were used in Africa and on the auction blocks in

America, were quickly dropped. This was meant to strip the slaves of their self-esteem by destroying culture, history, and individuality.

However, that was not exactly what happened. Denied their original cultures, slaves created a new culture, one that embraced their African pasts and accommodated their new status as captives. Along with this new culture—African-American culture—came a new oral tradition, one that would give rise to rap.

THE BLACK CHURCH The African-American oral tradition developed first and foremost with the slaves' adaption of the religion of their masters—Christianity. The services of the slaves were reminiscent of religious ceremonies in Africa. They were lively, uplifting affairs complete with music, chanting, and spiritual possessions (also known as "getting happy," or "getting the Spirit"). The high point of the service was the preacher's sermon, or call, and the congregation's response.

The slave preacher became the griot of this new land. He was expected to be a messenger and an entertainer. Nor was the congregation a passive party to "the Word." Ministers expected the congregation to interrupt their sermons with applause and affirmations of "Tell it like it is!" "Sho' you right," and "Preach!"

A silent congregation always made a slave preacher uncomfortable. While certain white religions viewed silence as a sign of respect for a minister's sermon, silence in a slave church meant that he was falling short in his delivery of God's message. If things got too unbearable, it was nothing for a preacher to ask his audience for a response by shouting, "Can I get a witness?" "Say amen, somebody!" or "Do ya'll hear me today?"

Centuries later and under different circumstances, rap and hip-hop (terms we'll use interchangeably throughout this book) would continue the tradition of call and response that began in slave churches with a crew encouraging a rapper (or hip-hop dancer) with "Go, 'head! Go 'head!" or "Word!"

DOUBLE MEANINGS Along with this practice of call and response, preachers in the black church filled their sermons with double meanings. Slave autobiographies indicate that many slave preachers did not preach a simple and seemingly safe message of submission. Slave preachers disguised messages of liberation in their recitation of biblical verses and in their figures of speech. When a preacher proclaimed that "ninety-nine and a half won't do," the masters assumed he was talking about fulfilling work tasks to the fullest. But the slaves knew that the preacher really meant never giving up the possibility of freedom.

Often slave church services were conducted under the watchful eyes, but usually untrained ears, of overseers or of masters themselves. Nevertheless, preachers were routinely accused of stirring slaves to revolt in the same manner that rappers like Ice Cube and Chuck D have been accused by politicians and others of encouraging unrest in today's inner cities.

FOLKTALES AND SPIRITUALS Double meanings abounded in entertaining slave folktales, often dismissed by whites as "darkie tales." The seemingly harmless stories of animals like Br'er Rabbit, Br'er Fox, and tar baby were full of inspirational messages for the slaves. The animals in these tales usually had very human qualities, and were often based on the personalities of those who ran and worked on plantations. These tales echoed the oratory of the African griots. Moreover, they commented on everyday life and frequently talked of freedom in ways that went over the heads of the slave masters.

Similarly, the spirituals and chants that the slaves created, often dismissed as "darkie songs," were powerful means of communication. A lyric like "I ain't got long to stay here," from the spiritual "Deep River," superficially meant that a slave was about to die and looked forward to life in the Promised Land, or Jordan. However, for many slaves, the song often signaled the local presence of Underground Railroad conductors like Harriet Tubman, who risked their lives to help courageous slaves escape the misery of bondage.

Quite unknowingly, the slave masters' attempts to divide and control blacks by censoring their speech only created and strengthened a new oral tradition and its ability to communicate ideas of freedom and unity. Throughout the time of slavery, it was a crime, punishable by death, for slaves to learn to read or write. Though many slaves did become literate, such restrictions forced most to be ingenious in their communications, and rely even more on what was already an intregral part of their heritage, the spoken word.

The griot, the slave preacher, and the storyteller all displayed a skillful use of language. The inherent African love of the spoken word, and the new way of life that America forced upon enslaved blacks set the stage for the black cultural explosion of the twentieth century—and the explosion of hip-hop.

chapter Two

Get On Up
The RiSe OF African-American Culture

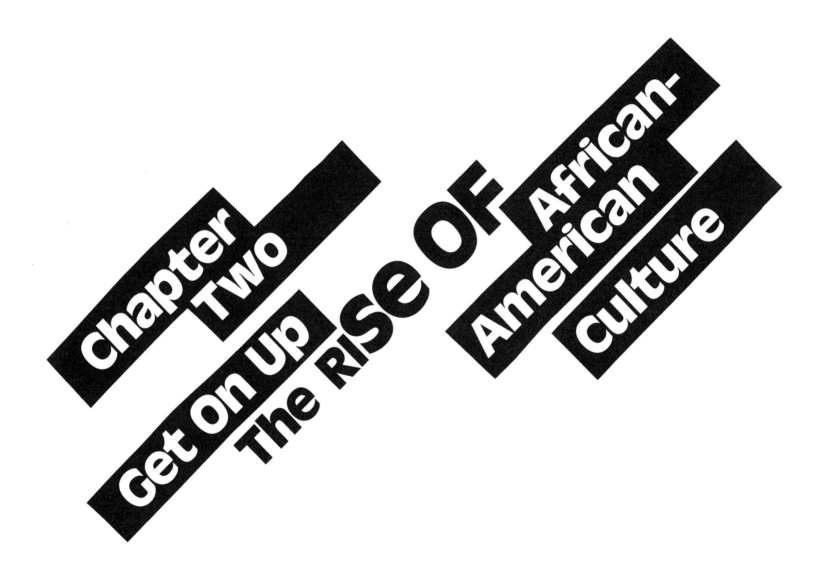

You will not be able to stay
home brother.
You will not be able to plug
in, turn on, and cop out.
The revolution will not be
brought to you by Xerox in
four parts with no commercial
interruptions.
The revolution will not give
your mouth sex appeal.
The revolution will not get
rid of the nubs.
The revolution will not make
you look five pounds thinner.
There will be no pictures of
pigs shooting down brothers on
instant replay.
There will be no highlights on
the eleven o'clock news.
The revolution will not be
right back after a message
from a white tornado, white
lightning, or white people.
The revolution will be live.

GIL SCOTT-HERON
"THE REVOLUTION WILL
NOT BE TELEVISED."[1]

When President Abraham Lincoln

issued the Emancipation Proclamation freeing slaves in 1863, there were some 4.5 million Africans living in the United States. All but 500,000 of these blacks had been slaves.

The Reconstruction Era, which lasted from 1866 to 1877, followed emancipation. The federal government, struggling to heal the nation in the aftermath of the Civil War, promised every newly emancipated adult black male—now referred to as a freedman—forty acres and a mule with which to begin a new life. It was a vow that was never fulfilled. (More than a century later, African-American filmmaker Spike Lee would ironically name his production company Forty Acres and a Mule Filmworks in remembrance of the government's broken promise to blacks. Reparations to African Americans for the economic and psychological exploitation they suffered as a result of slavery continued to be an issue widely discussed among African Americans during the 1990s.)

The majority of freedmen lived in the South. In order to survive, they traded the total bondage of slavery for the economic bondage of sharecropping—working on land they could never afford to own.

Until 1917, the livelihood of most blacks remained based in the agricultural South. But that year the United States entered World War I. As men in the industrialized North entered the armed forces and departed to fight in Europe, newly emerging industries needed factory workers. During the 1920s, 2 million blacks flowed from the South into urban areas such as Detroit, Chicago, St. Louis, and New

York in search of a better life through new jobs in factories. This movement was known as the Great Migration. As blacks entered these urban centers, the African-American oral and musical traditions that gave birth to rap developed at an astonishing rate.

BLUES, JAZZ, AND JIVE TALK About that time major record companies realized that there was money to be made from black culture and entertainment. Such record companies began to record what they called "race music," the work of musicians such as Jelly Roll Morton, the honky-tonk piano player; Bessie Smith, the "Empress of the Blues"; and W. C. Handy, the "Father of the Blues." Sold primarily to blacks, the blues told of the pain of the black experience, just as rap would more than seventy years later. Smith, Handy, and other stars toured the country playing before all-black audiences on the "chitlin' circuit." (The circuit, or route traveled by performers, was named after chitterlings, or hog intestines. During slavery, whites deemed these to be mere waste, but blacks turned them into a delicacy.)

The blues were communal and competitive. Singers often picked up one another's songs, rearranged them, and added new lyrics. (This practice was also found in the spirituals and gospel music.) Several generations later with the explosion of hip-hop, this tradition of communal ownership of melody and lyrics, when coupled with technology, would become known as sampling. Certain blues lyrics, moreover, like "Good morning blues, how do you do?" or "Believe half of what you see, and none of what you hear," appeared over and over in songs, just as James Brown's "Get on up!" appears in numerous raps. Although blues singers shared their material, they often tried to outdo each other in their interpretations of it. Many years later, rappers would also repeat the tradition of competition by rapping over the same backing tracks and samples.

The blues gave birth to jazz. Jazz began in big cities like Kansas City, St. Louis, Chicago, Detroit, New York, and New Orleans. Jazz was ironic, soulful, cool, colorful, and complex. Still, the music wasn't all about good times. It depicted the realities of life blacks faced: racism, poverty, and other social remnants from slavery days. When Thomas "Fats" Waller posed the musical question, "What did I do, to get so black and blue?," blacks understood his lyrics referred to the dangers of daily existence.

Jazz musicians like Louis Armstrong, Cab Calloway, and Louis Jordan mixed singing and the spoken word against the backdrop of their spectacular orchestras. When bandleader Cab Calloway hollered "Hi-Dee-Hi-Dee-Ho," in the refrain of "Minnie the Moocher," wildly appreciative audiences from Philadelphia to Paris shouted the words back at him. It was an updating of the call and response of the black church within the setting of secular music.

Yet jazz was more than music. It was a culture, an attitude, and a lifestyle. Jazz musicians created a vibrant speech, filled with smooth everyday rhythms, tall tales, wild-eyed rhymes, and sayings of black Americans. Musicians like Dizzy Gillespie concocted their own languages. Gillespie used words and phrases like "hep," "jive," "be-bop," "What you know, Daddy-O?" "Pucker up, buttercup," and "See you later, alligator."

But the creativity didn't stop there. Men like Gillespie, Charlie "Yardbird" Parker, Max Roach, Lester "Prez" Young, Philly Jo Jones, and Miles Davis set their own standards of dress and attitude. When certain musicians walked, they didn't merely walk, they bopped. Jazzmen generally had the reps, or reputations, of being among the world's most dapper dressers. The significance of such independence and self-definition would not be lost on hip-hop culture as rappers cut strong profiles and set fashion trends.

By the 1940s and 1950s, black disc jockeys were adding to the speech and style of jazz. With names like Dr. Jive, Tall Paul, the Ditty-Bop Pope, the Electrifying Mojo, The Queen, Jocko, the Chief Rocker, and The Love Bug, deejays attracted huge audiences in cities across the nation.

Between spinning records and during the instrumental breaks of songs, the deejays passed messages between lovers, commented on local affairs, and kept their listeners entertained with lines like: "Sounds so nice, I got to play it twice," or "As the clock on the rock chimes the time, I'm gonna make room for this hot new tune." Such talk became known as jive.

The jive and rhyming skills of the deejays had as much to do with their individual popularity as the records they were spinning. In this sense, they were the forefathers of the deejay/performer role that many early rappers assumed.

COMEDY AND THE DOZENS

While this new black culture of speech and music developed in the streets and over the airwaves, comedians were adding humor—very often some decidedly "low down and dirty" humor—to it. Funny men and women like Lawanda Page, Pigmeat Markham, Slappy White, Jackie "Moms" Mabley, Redd Foxx, Rudy

Ray Moore, and Richard Pryor combined wit, tall tales, innuendos, and social commentary in their routines. "We got to laugh to keep from crying," was a favorite expression among black comedians.

Early comedians usually performed as opening acts on the chitlin' circuit. Routines and monologues like Markham's "Here Come De Judge," Mabley's "Young Man," and Pryor's "Wino" kept audiences in stitches. In addition to humor and color, these comedians helped bring to popular black culture a sense of good-natured competition in their use of language. Comedians often had to think on their feet during shows, because at any point a member of the audience could interrupt a performance. In order to maintain control, the comedian had to silence hecklers with swift (and funny) verbal assaults. Their performances were often recorded and released as "party records." With little or no airplay or exposure to white audiences, such records nevertheless sold briskly.

Life in American cities sparked new word games within the black community that were keenly competitive. The most popular and enduring was the dozens. A ritual of urban African-American boys, the dozens was a good-natured vocal competition in which a boy made disparaging remarks about an opponent's mother. The dozens was always played with an audience, which encouraged the two opponents to outdo or "cap" on each other.

A typical dozens dual might go something like: "Your mother beat me so bad at basketball yesterday, I thought her name was Charles Barkley!" A comeback might be: "Your mamma slam dunk so tough, Nike's naming a sneaker after her!" The dozens required plenty of quick wit, imagination, exaggeration, and an artful use of profanity. Clichés just didn't cut it. Rappers like Biz Markie regularly opened a rap with a line like, "Your moms is so old that she knew Central Park when it was just a little tree."

All of these developments clearly were forerunners of the rap phenomenon. The bawdy humor of Biz Markie echoed the outrageousness of comedians on the chitlin' circuit. L.L. Cool J is always game for a verbal battle in the tradition of the dozens.

BLACK AND PROUD By the 1960s the boastfulness and competition that were a part of black culture had taken on newer, deeper meanings. A new sense of pride and self-assertiveness emerged among African Americans. At the forefront were black preachers. Ministers such as Reverend C. L. Franklin, (father of soul singer Aretha), Dr. Martin Luther King, Jr., the Rev. Jesse Jackson, and Malcolm X, among others, dazzled, inspired, and evoked white fear with their powerful oratories like "The Eagle Protects Her Nest," "By Any Means Necessary," and "A Drum Major for Justice." "The preacher is the most unique personality developed by the Negro on American soil," wrote civil rights activist and scholar W.E.B. Du Bois. "A leader, a politician, an orator. . . ."[2]

Franklin, the pastor of Detroit's New Bethel Baptist Church, was a pulpit legend. His sermons fused scripture, storytelling, and healthy doses of pride. When the Spirit "filled" Franklin, he would change from his regular speaking voice to what churchgoers called his "hooping" voice. Adopting a higher pitch, Franklin would vividly bring to life Bible stories such as the parable of the Prodigal Son: "He sat there among swines, with hogs all around him. Realizing, O Lord,

Images and Words from African-American Culture

This painting, *Afro Emblems* by African-American artist Hale Woodruff, uses patterns found in traditional African art, particularly ceremonial masks. Both knowingly and unknowingly, rappers have also continued artistic traditions that began in the "Motherland."

What is Africa to me:
Copper sun or scarlet sea,
Jungle star or jungle track,
Strong bronzed men,
  or regal black
Women from whose loins
  I sprang
When birds of Eden sang?
One three centuries removed
From the scenes his fathers
  loved . . .

COUNTEE CULLEN,
"HERITAGE"

An African mother and child (*right*) are sold into slavery in the American South. Enslaved blacks created the African-American oral and musical traditions that eventually gave rise to rap.

Fifty years after slavery ended, blacks migrated north to fill jobs left by whites who went to fight overseas during World War I. This Jacob Lawrence painting (*below*), from a series of canvases called *The Migration of the Negro*, shows blacks departing by train for northern cities.

Urban blacks created blues and jazz and expanded African-American culture, paving the way for rap. This Archibald Motley painting, *Gettin' Religion*, 1948, shows a preacher among jazz musicians on a city street.

Oh, summer summer
  summertime—
Then grim street preachers
  shook
their tambourines and Bibles
  in the face
of tolerant wickedness;
then Elks parades and big
  splendiferous
Jack Johnson in his diamond
  limousine
set the ghetto burgeoning
with fantasies
of Ethiopia spreading her
  gorgeous wings.
          ROBERT HAYDEN,
            " 'SUMMERTIME AND THE LIVING . . .' "

Bessie Smith, Empress of the Blues. Independent, strong, successful, she provided a model for black women entertainers of many eras—from singer Billie Holiday to rapper Queen Latifah.

There ain't nothin' I can do, or nothin' I can say, that folks don't criticize me. But I'm going to do as I want to anyway, and don't care if they all despise me.
BESSIE SMITH,
" 'T'AIN'T NOBODY'S BIZNESS IF I DO"

W.E.B. Du Bois, shown in this portrait by Laura Waring (*left*), influenced generations of black thinkers, writers, and rappers. During the early twentieth century, Du Bois published powerful meditations on race and black history, such as *The Souls of Black Folk*.

. . . [T]he Negro is a sort of seventh son, born with a veil, and gifted with second-sight in this American world, — a world which yields him no true self-consciousness, but only lets him see himself through the revelation of the other world. It is a peculiar sensation, this double-consciousness, this sense of always looking at one's self through the eyes of others, of measuring one's soul by the tape of a world that looks on in amused contempt and pity. One ever feels his two-ness, — an American, a Negro; two souls, two thoughts, two unreconciled strivings, two warring ideals in one dark body, whose dogged strength alone keeps it from being torn asunder.

W.E.B. DU BOIS,
"OF OUR SPIRITUAL STRIVINGS," *THE SOULS OF BLACK FOLK*

Charles White's *Preacher*. Key figures in holding together black communities since the days of slavery, black preachers and religious leaders took on even greater importance as the twentieth century progressed. Men like the Reverend Dr. Martin Luther King, Jr., mobilized blacks for political change. Their sermons and speeches embodied the best of the African-American oral tradition of which rap is a part.

Malcolm X speaking at a rally
commemorating Marcus Garvey.
Probably no other black leader was
more important to rap. His messages
of black pride and self-determination
appeared in thousands of songs as
rappers sampled his speeches.

Malcolm, flaming cosmic spirit
  who walks
amongst us, we hear your voice
speaking wisdom in the wind,
we see your vision in the life/fires
  of men,
who watched your image
flaming in the sun
        QUINCY TROUPE,
          "FOR MALCOLM X WHO WALKS IN
          THE EYES OF OUR CHILDREN"

The beats that singer James Brown (*right*) and his band created during the late 1960s became the most sampled in rap. The snare drum solo on "Funky Drummer" alone fueled songs by everyone from Irish singer Sinead O'Connor to Public Enemy, which took its name from a Brown composition. George Clinton (*below*). The pioneering funk he recorded during the 1970s and 1980s also supplied the music of rap.

Uncle George passed the funk sign to me, which I gave to all the hip-hoppers throughout the world. Uncle George is the baddest, coolest, meanest, stylin'est, jazziest, hottest, wildest, Lord of Universal Funk. May he live on 4 ever, because we want the funk and the funk is hip-hop.

AFRIKA BAMBAATAA

The legendary Jamaican deejay U-Roy (*right*). U-Roy chanted rhythmically or "toasted" over the records he spun. Toasting gave birth to rap when other Jamaican deejays— influenced by U-Roy— came to New York City.

Rap drew on all of African-American culture. This Charles Searles painting *Feles for Sale* features the colorful skullcaps, *feles*. Originating in Nigeria, feles became a rap fashion, symbolizing rap's union of African and American elements.

my black mother is a long-haired
  sensuous river
where the Kongo flows into the
  Mississippi she
is coming where my father's blood
  rises in jets
and like rain, glows, transformed red,
  tan, black
I am growing in the bosom and
  in the loins
of America
born and knitted in the soil, when
  I finish growing
you can pick me as you would a
  rare and fabulous
seed and you can
blow Africa on me
as you would a holy reed.

HENRY DUMAS,
"AFRO-AMERICAN"

great God, that he'd sought a freedom without laws. You ought to be able to see him, just sitting there thinking to himself: Here I am in rags, tattered rags."[3] Franklin's oratory was so powerful that even the most worldly members of his audience considered giving their lives to Christ.

Beginning in the 1920s, more flamboyant ministers bestowed names upon themselves like Daddy Grace, Father Divine, and Prophet Jones. Sermons like "Route 66" provided an overview of the sixty-six books of the Bible and made inventive use of the name of the famous cross-country U.S. highway. Both in their delivery and in personality, such preachers dazzled.

THE GREATEST Razzle-dazzle was something that a young fighter from Louisville, Kentucky, knew all about. From the time of his professional boxing debut in 1964, it was obvious that Cassius Clay, who would later join the Nation of Islam and change his name to Muhammad Ali, was no ordinary athlete. Clay did not follow in the footsteps of older Negro sports superstars like track-and-field wonder Jesse Owens, former heavyweight boxing champion Joe Louis, or Jackie Robinson, major league baseball's first black player. Many whites condescendingly considered each of these athletes "a credit to his race." Clay seemed determined to rock the boat and discard the notion of being a "nice Negro."

Clay was blessed with dashing good looks, a spectacular shuffle that left his opponents dizzy, and a knockout punch. Charisma was in his sweat — and Clay knew it. But that wasn't good enough. Clay wanted the world to know that he was "pretty" and "the greatest."

Through incredible bragging and recitation of self-penned poetry, motormouth Clay hyped his talents even further. His verses weren't filled with the flowery language some Americans found poetic. Instead, his poems dripped with the street-corner sayings and pulpit phrases of black America. The same brashness would be displayed years later by Ali's hip-hop grandson, L.L. Cool J.

Never before had someone who didn't fit the traditional definition of a poet so clearly put the poetic everyday speech of black Americans in the white mainstream, or on "front street," as they said in the ghetto. Clay, a master instigator, was as deadly with a rhyme as he was with his fists. He taunted opponents with proclamations like: "I float like a butterfly and sting like a bee." He even went as far as predicting (in rhyme) the round in which his opponent would fall. And then he delivered!

Clay captured the heart of America. However, his conversion to the controversial religion of the Nation of Islam and subsequent name change further intensified the spotlight into which he thrust himself.

When he refused induction into the military during the Vietnam War in 1967, Ali faced his greatest challenge. He was stripped of his heavyweight title. Four years later he reclaimed it. Throughout his exile and battles with the government, Ali retained his composure.

Ali's acclaim as an extraordinary athlete was universal. Yet, his political resolve represented many things to many people. For many blacks, he was a symbol of pride and independence. To many whites, his belief in Islam and his mouth qualified him as "uppity." Yet, he stood up to the system. Ali exposed America to the power of a strong black man and the wonderful oral tradition of his community. In this sense, he was one of rap's forefathers.

POWER, PANTHERS, AND POETRY During the same period, the Black Power movement was gaining momentum among younger blacks. Activists like H. "Rap" Brown—whose nickname came from his extraordinary verbal ability—and Stokely Carmichael openly questioned the conservative, nonviolent, middle-class, and Christian philosophies of leaders like Martin Luther King, Jr. Brown, Carmichael, and other young militants spoke directly to poor blacks in America's ghettos. They created slogans like "Quit looting and start shooting," and "Burn, baby, burn," during the civil disorders that erupted across the United States in the 1960s. These bold, politically charged statements would later inspire rappers like Paris, Ice-T, and KRS-One to confront established authority with depictions of urban poverty, illiteracy, and violence.

The sixties inspired equally candid literary expression among black writers and poets. The Last Poets, a group of former convicts, brought the street wisdom of young inner-city men to national attention with searing performances like "Niggers Are Scared of Revolution," and "White Man's Got a God Complex." The Last Poets' recitations painted brutal scenarios of black American life and were usually accompanied by drums and occasionally a bass.

Broadside Press, a small publishing company based in Detroit, Michigan, showcased the works of many of the country's most prolific young black writers. Poets like Don L. Lee (now Haki Madhubuti), Sonia Sanchez, and Nikki Giovanni wrote and recited poetry in the language of young blacks. In the poem "Ego Tripping (There May Be a Reason Why)," Giovanni traversed the history of ancient Africa and Europe with the same finesse, confidence, and humor that would later characterize the verses of Queen Latifah.

I gave my son Hannibal an elephant
He gave me Rome for Mother's Day
My strength flows ever on
My son Noah built a new
ark and I stood proudly at the helm as we sailed
*   on a soft summer day*
I turned myself into myself and was Jesus
Men intone my loving name
All praises All praises
I am the one who would save[4]

Poets like Giovanni removed the dual meanings from their verses. In blaring, blatant, and egotistical terms they both proclaimed the beauty of their blackness and their rejection of the norms and values imposed upon blacks by white Americans. At readings, Giovanni and Lee evoked emotions similar to those preachers did.

More than any other literary figure of the late 1960s and early 1970s, Gil Scott-Heron bridged the gap between the oral and musical traditions of black Americans. Whereas other artists either sang or recited exclusively, Heron did both. Heron's works, such as "The Revolution Will Not Be Televised," were actually a combination of poetry, song, social commentary, and the everyday language of the black community.

"Black people everywhere are becoming aware of the gap that exists between American values and the values of our spirits," Heron, son of a Chicago librarian and a professional Jamaican soccer star, wrote in the liner notes of his 1972 album *Free Will*. "What we need is self-love and respect. Unfortunately it is not easy to love yourself after years of self-hatred. We see evidence of self-hatred and self-destruction in every city. We must make the extra effort needed to identify the true enemies of our peace and peace of mind."

Like the generation of rappers that would follow him, Heron's popularity spread, not through radio airplay, but by word of mouth. "I see myself as a modern day version of the African Griot," Heron said.[5]

THE GODFATHER For rap, the most profound musician of the 1960s was Soul Brother Number One, the Godfather of Soul, the Hardest Working Young Man in Show Business, Mr. Dynamite, Mr. Please, Please, Please—James Brown. Born in Augusta, Georgia, Brown began his rise to popularity as a typical, straight-hair-wearing rhythm and blues singer during the 1950s. Brown's live shows (or revues) were distinct in their nonstop music, dancing, and raw energy. He was without peer. (Years later, Hammer attempted to copy the frenetic atmosphere of Brown's productions in his extravagant stage shows and videos.) Like a preacher delivering a sermon, Brown half-shouted and half-sang his songs.

Brown was the star of his self-named revue. However, the presence and participation of his supporting cast was equally as important. Like the slave preachers a century before calling on their congregations, Brown often shouted to his band, the JBs, for help directing songs during performances, with phrases like, "Can I hit it and quit?" Bandleaders Maceo Parker and Fred Wesley, who often harmonized, talked jive, or took extended solos during Brown's shows and on record, were celebrated sidekicks. Years later in hip-hop culture such entourages would emerge as posses or crews. As always, the call and response of the oral tradition provided the model.

Brown's early hits like "Cold Sweat," and "Mother Popcorn" were mainly about romance or dance crazes. By 1967, Brown had traded in his straightened hair for an Afro, or "natural" hairstyle. His song lyrics changed as well. They began to reflect the self-determination and pride that was sweeping black America. This was evident in songs like "I Don't Want Nobody to Give Me Nothing (Open Up the Door, I'll Get It Myself)," and "Say It Loud (I'm Black and I'm Proud)." On the latter song Brown served notice in a rap that the revolution was not about to cease:

> *Some say we got a lot of malice,*
> *Some say we got a lot of nerve,*
> *I say we won't stop,*
> *until we get what we deserve.*
> *Say it Loud,*
> *I'm black and I'm proud!* [6]

Equally as important as Brown's words was his backbeat. The rhythms and riffs created by Brown, Wesley, and Parker would become among the most sampled beats in rap.

THE CARIBBEAN The Black Power movement in the United States did not go unnoticed by blacks elsewhere in the Americas, who had also come to this hemisphere as slaves. Jamaicans and Trinidadians, in particular, paid attention to culture and political developments in black America, and blended them with their own experiences. They used their own unique variations of English, or *patois*, to express themselves in speech and music.

In the sixties, Jamaican deejays, or "selectors," began traversing the island nation with massive "sound systems." These outfits usually consisted of large flatbed trucks armed with mountains of turntables, speakers and amplifiers, all powered by generators, that blasted the latest American and Jamaican tunes for all within hearing distance to enjoy. The major "sound system men" of this era were Duke Reid and Sir Coxsonne.

Selectors favored tunes that resonated with bass and drums, or were dub versions — the instrumental flipsides of local popular hits, usually of ska or rock steady tunes, which were the musical forerunners of reggae. To further entertain the audience, the deejay would "toast" or talk over the records. A typical toast might go something like: "This generation will rock the nation with version!"

Toasting would evolve into dancehall, the Jamaican equivalent of rap. And the traveling sound systems would boom on the streets of America's cities as young hip-hoppers blared their music in public on portable music systems called boom boxes, or ghetto blasters, and in the stereos of Jeeps, the status cars of rap.

Jamaican dub poets like Mutaburuka and Michael Smith were similar in delivery and tone to Gil Scott-Heron and the Broadside poets. Reciting poetry over a slow, steady drum and bass groove and more uptempo roots reggae, the dub poets critiqued conditions plaguing Africans throughout the world from apartheid in South Africa and the effects of the Cold War on global politics, to local concerns like housing and police brutality. "Jamaica's deejays serve as the nation's street poets, oracles and phrasemakers," music journalists Stephen Davis and Peter Simon noted.[7]

The subject matter of Jamaican-born, British-raised dub poet Linton Kwesi Johnson typifies the form. "De eagle and de bear have people living in fear of impending nuclear warfare," Linton spoke in "De Eagle & De Bear," referring to the Soviet Union and the United States who were, at the time, engaged in a nuclear arms race.[8]

In Trinidad, calypso musicians, called calypsonians, displayed many of the same cultural attributes as the West African griots and the black American preachers, poets, and musicians. Artists like Attila the Hun, Shadow, the Mighty Sparrow, and Lord Kitchener were legendary for their ability to assemble a witty combination of verses on the spot. Their words were never gibberish, but usually a biting commentary on local or international events.

Each year calypsonians held center stage in Trinidadian culture from the Christmas season through the celebration of carnival in mid-February. During that time they engaged in nightly verbal competitions known as calypso tent, for the coveted title of Road March King.

The tradition dated back to the fifteenth century and was part of Trinidad's legacy of slavery, under both the French and the British. Carnival was the one time of year when slaves were permitted to openly criticize and mock their colonial masters and owners, usually in the form of satire.

The calypso tent competitions were fierce, and entailed nightly runoffs in which contestants, in addition to having catchy, rhythmic tunes, knocked off their fellow contestants. The winner was determined by audience response. Many times during competitions, a tie could only be broken by *picong*. Picong was an impromptu verbal dual between two calypsonians. No music was involved.

A spinoff of calypso was *rapso*—the Trinidadian counterpart of toasting. Journalist Chako Habekost wrote:

Rapso developed toward the end of the 1970s, around the same time as dub poetry. Fueled by the period of social unrest and political activism, rapso became the mouthpiece of the underprivileged masses of Trinidad & Tobago. Its birthplace is the shanty town of East Dry River, which for decades was the breeding ground for militant political actions and an explosive cultural creativity.[9]

One of rapso's leading figures, Brother Resistance, had no qualms about the origins and purpose of his art form:

I come to rock every room in yuh conscience,
to beat off de chain dat imprison yuh brain,
I ride dis riddum from de heart of resistance
and who see or hear well
dey must feel de pain.
For de time has come when every heart
go tremble to de riddum of de drum.[10]

The calypsonians, like the griots before them and the rappers to follow them, were the standard-bearers of an oral tradition. Trinidadian playwright Mustapha Matura told a *New York Times* reporter:

In Trinidad, language is a way people entertain themselves. After all, there isn't much else to do. The better you are with words, the more status you acquire. I'm not talking about educated people, but ordinary people who, through using their imagination, develop gifts for language. Humor and wit are prized qualities among Trinidadians.[11]

In the 1970s the Caribbean and African-American oral traditions would meet in New York City. And when they did, rap was born.

CHAPTER THREE

Back in the Day

Now what you hear is not a test—I'm rappin' to the beat.

And me, the groove, and my friends are gonna try to move your feet.

But first I gotta bang bang the boogie to the boogie.

Say hip-hop, you don't stop.

Say up jump to boogies to the bang bang boogies

Let's rock, you don't stop.

THE SUGAR HILL GANG
"RAPPER'S DELIGHT"[1]

The year was 1978.

American music, at least on the radio, was flat. The dull thud of disco dominated the airwaves. Popularized by groups like the Village People, and the Bee Gees, disco sounded as if it were constructed by robots or computers, not created by human beings.

The soulful 1960s had given way to a much more impersonal music. The quality of disco was measured not by lyrics, melody, or artistic performance but rather by the number of mechanically produced beats per minute that it contained. And beyond the dance floor, disco had no bearing in reality.

YOUNG MCS The brothers up in New York City's South Bronx weren't having it. The rejection of disco by inner-city youth was the final stage in the birth of rap. Bored with the artificial thud they heard on the radio, black kids began rummaging through their parents' record collections in search of a beat to party to. They weren't disappointed. The music of James Brown, Kool and the Gang, Sly Stone, George Clinton, Curtis Mayfield, the Jimmy Castor Bunch, and other soulmen of the 1960s and 1970s still sounded good.

Two Bronx deejays, DJ Hollywood and DJ Kool Herc, who would eventually be hailed as the founding fathers of rap, agreed. Jamaican-born Herc immigrated to New York City in 1969 when he was twelve years old. By that age, he had already been influenced by the style of Jamaican toasters like Big Youth, I-Roy, Prince Far-I, U-Roy, Dillinger, and their numerous sound systems. In America his ears filled with the fast talk of black radio deejays.

In 1975 Herc started deejaying at Bronx teen clubs, community centers, and parties. At his gigs Herc began spinning short sections of different records and talking over them. But the innovations of Herc and other deejays didn't stop there. Soon Herc played records on two turntables at the same time. With the aid of a sound mixer that allowed him to fade in and out between records, Herc developed the technique of mixing passages from one song into another. He would pick the most recognizable part of a hit or a soul classic and play it over and over again, integrating pieces of others songs while rhyming over them.

Herc became notorious for incorporating the most obscure records into his mixes. Anything was fair game for inclusion in a mix: a James Brown scream, a Wilson Pickett grunt, a funky bass line, a guitar riff, and even tidbits of jingles and theme songs from popular TV shows and movies. Soon partygoers were showing up at halls and clubs just to check out what the deejays were "dropping" on the mic and the turntable.

But as deejays like Herc refined such an approach, they saw that it demanded two distinct, highly skilled activities at the same time. Mixing music required great research, concentration, and precision. At the same time, rhyming required better-than-average verbal skills and the ability to improvise—particularly in a community where call and response was the norm. Any MC (or master of ceremonies, as rappers began to call themselves) with lame rhymes could be booed off the mike by a rowdy audience, just as a slow-talking comedian on the chitlin' circuit had been. "An MC can't walk out of his door without a rhyme," said Casual of Hieroglyphics. "You always have to be ready. Rapping is like a game of one-on-one basketball. If I go up against you, not only am I going to try and beat you, I'm going to try and embarrass you."[2]

A division of labor was required. Deejays began concentrating on mixing party music. MCs began to approach their rhymes, chants, and monologues with the dedication of scientists. Thus the rap phrase "dropping science" was born.

Competition was keen among deejays and MCs. It didn't matter if they were performing at house parties, block parties, on the playground, or at paying events. Deejays and MCs knew that they had to "throw down" to maintain their reps.

No longer content to simply spin records, deejays were always looking for new ways to outdo each another. Soon the technique of "scratching" was developed. Scratching involved manually moving a spinning record on a turntable back and forth over select passages. It created one of rap's signature sounds.

Early MCs recognized the importance of paying their respects to the audience. It was commonplace for MCs to acknowledge family, friends, and community big shots with chants like "Mike Cash is in the house! Jimmy D is in the house! The Bronx is in the house!" Such courtesies would become part of rap etiquette. But they were more than obligatory greetings, they were a part of community rituals in black culture.

THE BREAKS In the summer of 1979, rap broke out big time. A trio of unknowns who called themselves the Sugar Hill Gang unleashed "Rapper's Delight" on an unsuspecting America. Until "Rapper's Delight," a nonstop fourteen-minute-ten-second rhyme romp over the rhythm and melody of "Good Times," a huge dance hit by the group Chic, rap was primarily an art form of the moment. Deejays and MCs became ghetto celebrities by selling cheaply made cassette recordings of their mixes and live shows. However, nobody's raps had been preserved on vinyl until "Delight" kicked open the doors of opportunity.

The Sugar Hill Gang was brought together by Sylvia Robinson, a former soul singer. Robinson founded Sugar Hill Records, named after the fashionable Harlem neighborhood that boasted doctors, lawyers, and ministers among its residents. It was Robinson's business to keep her ears open for new talent. She often overheard her teenagers talking about the verbal abilities of MCs who ruled the weekend party circuit in New York City.

One day in a pizza parlor she overheard an employee, MC Big Bank Hank, talking in rhymes as he went about his work. She asked him if he'd be interested in recording his rap. Why not, Hank replied.

Hank teamed up with two other rappers, and a sensation was born. "Rapper's Delight" sold over 500,000 copies and hit number one on the pop music charts. The term "hip-hop" and other enduring rap phrases such as "Let me hear you say, ho" also came out of the song.

A few months later Kurtis Blow, another Sugar Hill artist, released "Christmas Rappin'," which sold nearly a million copies. His next single "The Breaks" was a good-natured look at Murphy's Law:

If your woman steps out with another man,
(That's the breaks, that's the breaks)
And she runs off with him to Japan,

And the IRS says they want to chat,
And you can't explain why you claimed your cat,
And you borrowed money from the mob,
And yesterday you lost your job,
Well, these are the breaks.[3]

Another pivotal force in the early days of rap was Afrika Bambaataa and his Zulu Nation. Bambaataa was a Bronx street deejay who spun records at block parties and in the parks. But unlike other deejays who were strictly party animals, Bambaataa incorporated a strong element of cultural awareness into his presentations.

A former gang member, Bambaataa schooled himself in the philosophies of black nationalist leaders like Marcus Garvey and Malcolm X. He saw music as a way to unify ghetto youth. A stocky, chocolate man, Bambaataa styled himself after Shaka, the great Zulu king and warrior of what became South Africa. In turn, his youth group, which was known for its musical and dancing abilities, became known as the Zulu Nation.

Bambaataa was accepted as a unifying force in an area that was plagued by turf wars between youth gangs. His deejay and MC skills were exceptional. His presentations were a cultural patchwork. Bambaataa might open his show with something far-fetched like the theme song from the 1960s television show "The Andy Griffith Show," which he had literally taped off of his television. Certainly, nothing could be further from the reality of a party on the tough streets of the Bronx than a piece of music associated with a group of rural whites residing in the fictitious town of Mayberry, U.S.A. But therein lay the brilliance of Bambaataa's work. He pushed the limits of cultural and musical association by mixing the shotgun horns or drum beats of a James Brown or Junior Walker tune with the Andy Griffith theme song.

BEYOND THE BRONX Punk rockers were the first group outside the ghetto to acknowledge rap. Fab 5 Freddy, a struggling Harlem-born artist who later became the host of the show *Yo! MTV Raps*, was a pivotal figure in bridging the gap between the worlds of punk and rap. As Freddy hung out in New York's bohemian East Village art circles, he noted that many young white artists were curious about black culture. He began booking rap performances into trendy New Wave clubs and art galleries. The response was tremendous. Hip whites celebrated the art of Bambaataa and Grandmaster Flash when Freddy introduced them to it.

Rap's first non-ghetto acknowledgment came from the punk-rock group Blondie. Their international smash "Rapture" spotlighted rap. Midway through the punk/funk jam, lead vocalist Debbie Harry broke into a science-fiction rap about a man from Mars, "eating cars and eating bars." Harry, exhibiting the etiquette of an MC, also credited Fab 5 Freddy for exposing her to this new form of music: "Fab 5 Freddy told me everybody's fly/Dee-jay spinnin', I said, 'My My.'" However, Harry's rap concluded with the distinctly non-uptown lyric: "don't stop, do punk rock."[4]

Such words hardly put rap on the map in terms of mainstream American culture, but they certainly acknowledged its existence for music lovers beyond Harlem and the Bronx. Still, the music industry wasn't yet ready to take rap seriously. To many, the music industry's initial dismissal of rap was laced with racism. In addition to assuming that rap was just a fad (years earlier similar assumptions had been made about blues, jazz, and soul music) many industry executives assumed that this creation by poor black kids from New York's ghettos was "too raw," "too ethnic" and "too street" to really gain mass popularity. How wrong and shortsighted the skeptics were to assume that they could determine rap's significance.

Chapter Four
THE MESSAGE SPREADS

It's like a jungle sometimes, it makes me wonder
How I keep from going under.
Broken glass everywhere,
People pissing on the stairs,
You know they just don't care.
I can't take the smell, can't take the noise,
Got no money to move out, I guess I got no choice.
Don't push me 'cause I'm close to the edge
I'm trying not to lose my head.

GRANDMASTER FLASH
AND THE FURIOUS FIVE
"THE MESSAGE"[1]

Until
Grandmaster
Flash dropped "The Message" in 1982, rappers were primarily concerned with having a good time. "When rap first started, it was strictly party music," the Fresh Prince (aka Will Smith) noted. "It was all about let's have some fun, and let the crowd scream over some music. Then real poets, like Chuck D and Rakim, started to find rap as a way of expression."[2]

Partying obviously wasn't what Grandmaster Flash's Melle Mel had in mind in "The Message." His rap painted a dismal, graphic picture of life in America's slums. The rap's effect was comparable to that of any newscast or documentary.

Mainstream America, then two years into the conservative Reagan-Bush era, simply ignored tales from the slums. Nevertheless, the modern-day griots told their stories. With amazing speed, rap began to diversify and multiply. Before long, listeners could choose between the party-down braggadocio of old-school rappers like Kurtis Blow; b-boys — rap terminology for macho men — like L.L. Cool J; the black nationalism of Public Enemy, the gangster rap of Ice-T, and others.

"Everybody has something that they want to say," observed Will Smith. "Everybody has different styles. Look at rap just like you look at movies. Different filmmakers have different opinions, and different attitudes."

Rap's variety has always been a reflection of its varied creators. PG rappers like the Fresh Prince or Young MC come from backgrounds that are very different from those of a group like the Geto

Boys, natives of Houston's notorious Fifth Ward. Similarly, because of the New York City–Jamaican immigrant connection, it was logical that KRS-One should incorporate dancehall toasting into his hip-hop. Rappers connected with each other as often as they contradicted each other.

"In rap, it's about being yourself," said Will Smith. And with rare exception, each rapper in his or her own way continued the tradition of the griot.

B-BOYS AND SEX SYMBOLS Run-D.M.C. became rap's first superstars. This duo of rappers, Darryl McDaniels (D.M.C.) and Joseph Simmons (Run), and a deejay, Jason Mizell (Jam Master Jay), came from Hollis, Queens, a section of New York City. The trio's image rejected many of raps norms. They performed in street clothes. Run, D.M.C., and Jam Master Jay swaggered on stage in unlaced high-top sneakers, black Kangol hats (then required gear for rappers), and warm-up jackets. The three were rap's pioneer b-boys.

Like their look, Run-D.M.C.'s music and message were stripped down and basic:

War going on across the sea,
Street soldiers killing the elderly,
Whatever happened to unity?
It's like that and that's the way it is.[3]

Run-D.M.C. also demonstrated that they were wordsmiths by giving tongue twisters and nursery rhymes a street slant:

Now Peter Piper picked peppers, but Run rocked rhymes.
Humpty Dumpty fell down, now that's his hard times.[4]

At first, other rap groups ridiculed, or dissed, Run-D.M.C. for their simplicity. But Run-D.M.C. had something the others didn't. They broke many barriers for rap, and became living legends. Pop fans went wild over the group's pairing with aging rockers Aerosmith for a rap remake of the rock tune "Walk This Way." (The collaboration jump-started Aerosmith's stalled career, making the band one of the biggest acts of the late 1980s and early 1990s.) They were the first rap group to appear on the TV show *American Bandstand*, a Saturday afternoon institution of white American pop music, and on MTV. They earned rap's first platinum album and were the first rappers to appear on the Grammy Awards. And they even starred in two movies, *Krush Groove* and *Tougher than Leather*.

Like Run-D.M.C., L.L. Cool J hailed from the middle class. Born James Todd Smith in 1968, L.L. Cool J (which stands for Ladies Love Cool James) was a star from the moment he dropped his first single "I Can't Live Without My Radio." The rap reflected the importance of music to African-American youth. "Radio" was the kind of jam meant to be played loud, or as L.L. raps, with the volume "way past 10."[5]

L.L. was a chest-thumper in the tradition of Muhammad Ali:

Cool J exists as a journalist,
Illuminate over any number on the Richter,
My throat contracts like a boa constrictor,
Dialect so def, it'll rip up the floor,
Ignite and excite with verbal extensions.[6]

For all their talent, rappers like Run-D.M.C. and L.L. Cool J risked losing their "street" credibility with their ghetto fans. In rap, as in other forms of the black oral tradition, the ideas and the language must be kept fresh. Feisty up-and-coming rappers began to criticize D.M.C. and Cool J on record. They accused the rappers, who were successful or "living large," of losing touch with the ghettos. The excessiveness of L.L. Cool J's thick gold chains and gaudy five-knuckle rings wasn't cool, or "down," anymore. When the Adidas company marketed a line of Run-D.M.C. footwear, black kids steered clear of the sneaker. The youth of America's black ghettos were looking for something new. New griots awaited them.

FIGHT THE POWER   Public Enemy filled the gap in 1987. Coming live and direct from the New York suburb of Long Island, which they dubbed "Strong Island," Public Enemy took their name from a popular antidrug song by James Brown, "Public Enemy Number One." The group's concept was the brainchild of college student Chuck D (aka Carlton Ridenhour). Ridenhour wanted to form a rap group that had a black nationalist message. At the same time, he wanted the group's music to move and groove people. From jump street, P.E. was the antithesis of the popular rappers of the day. They did not sport gaudy jewelry, and had little use for the comedic antics of a rap group like the Fat Boys. "It's about gold brains now, not gold chains," Chuck D explained to journalist Bill Adler.[7]

P.E. was dead serious and looked as provocative as they sounded. Their stage show included the Security of the First World

(S1Ws) sporting military fatigues and brandishing fake Uzis. The image was based on the Fruit of Islam, the security force of the Nation of Islam, and the militant, well-armed Black Panthers of the 1960s. "P.E. wants to reconvene the black power movement with hip-hop as the medium," explained hip-hop journalist Greg Tate.[8]

"When Run was jumping around rapping about 'at the age of four,' rap was okay," said rapper and producer Easy Mo Bee. "Then here comes Chuck D, and all of a sudden there's a problem. Rap becomes political, and the only people who really worried about it were white people, or anyone else who had a guilty conscience."[9]

P.E.'s lyrics confronted, in the language of the streets, the legacy of racism in America:

Most of my heroes don't appear on no stamps.
Sample a look back, you look and find
Nothin' but rednecks for 400 years if you check.[10]

There were no taboos in P.E.'s thought-provoking lyrics. Their raps criticized black-on-black violence:

A Black hand
Squeezed on Malcolm X the man.[11]

They were accused of being anti-Semitic:

Crucifixion ain't no fiction
So called chosen, frozen

Apology made to whoever pleases
Still they got me like Jesus.[12]

In the highly controversial rap and video "By the Time I Get to Arizona," Chuck D and company contemplated the assassination of the governor of the only state in the Union that refused to acknowledge Martin Luther King's birthday as a national holiday. P.E.'s albums bore provocative titles like *Fear of a Black Planet* and *Apocalypse '91: The Empire Strikes Black.*

For all of P.E.'s political daring, some critics found the group insensitive. Raps that advocated violence against women and gays led some Americans to wonder if Chuck D was really as sophisticated as his antiracism raps indicated.

KRS-One (Kris Parker) and Boogie Down Production were P.E.'s colleagues of consciousness and controversy. Parker, a product of the South Bronx, has been perhaps one of the most articulate voices in rap. Like many rappers, KRS-One (which stands for Knowledge Reigns Supreme Over Nearly Everyone) was a self-made man. A homeless youth, for several years he lived in New York City shelters. After dropping out of school at age thirteen, Parker spent his time in the Manhattan public library, devouring the books of Ivan Van Sertima, John Henrik Clarke, Lerone Bennett, Jr., and other black scholars and philosophers.

At one of the shelters, Parker befriended a young social worker named Scott Sterling, who moonlighted as deejay Scott LaRock. The two men discovered their mutual love of music. In short order they formed their own version of a Jamaican sound system, Boogie Down

Productions (BDP). The system was named in honor of the borough in which they formed their partnership, the "boogie down" Bronx.

Their first single, "Crack Attack," hit the streets in 1986 and became a massive ghetto hit. Unfortunately, Scott LaRock was killed while trying to break up an argument in the Bronx in 1987. KRS-One was determined that LaRock's legacy would live on through BDP.

KRS-One became known for his raps that advocated unity and awareness among black youth:

> *Some people say I am a rap missionary,*
> *Some people say I am a walking dictionary,*
> *Some people say I am truly legendary,*
> *But what I am is simply a black revolutionary.*[13]

KRS-One solidified his position as an MC who could kick a rhyme and impart a cultural message. "I'm concerned about the kids who don't know what time it is," Parker said, using a rap phrase for being wise.[14] He developed a reputation as a unifier within the hip-hop community. Through the National Urban League, Parker helped organize the Stop the Violence project. Aimed at urban youth, the project was a plea from the rap community for their audiences to forsake violence. Another project, Human Education Against Lies (HEAL), was dedicated to increasing literacy among ghetto youth.

In many ways, KRS-One was the Malcolm X of rap. He blasted the inferior public school systems of America's inner cities, and urged his young fans to supplement their learning with the works of noted black scholars such as W.E.B. Du Bois. Parker terms his style of rap "edutainment," a combination of education and entertainment:

I sit in your unknown class while you're failing us.
I failed your class 'cause I ain't with your reasoning.
You try to make me you by seasoning.
Mess up my mind with 'See Jane run, See John walk'
in a hard-core New York.
It doesn't exist, no way, no how.
It's like a chocolate cow.[15]

"Most kids in schools are disinterested," Parker, who lectures at high schools and colleges, observed. "They're probably just throwing paper. But if they start to read material that teaches them about themselves, they expand. They become part of intellectual gangs. Then they'll meaningfully start to question authority. Most rappers can't talk about nothing but gold chains, cars, and blowing people away. That's all their vocabulary is. But in my lectures, I encourage kids to read the dictionary as they'd read a book. That way they will understand what the English language is all about."

Parker's lectures gave rap a decidedly funky, academic bent, which he expanded even further. He wrote editorials for *The New York Times* on homelessness and the importance of black history. He also rejected the image of "living large," which many rappers played to the hilt by endorsing products like fast food, sneakers, and beer. "My [political] position weeds a lot of people out," he acknowledged. "The people who ain't down with me, I ain't down with them. There's no way I'm going to compromise my message."[16]

THE ICE MEN COMETH While KRS-One rapped about the lessons learned from black scholars, gangster rappers rapped about the lessons they learned from the streets. Gangster rap explored the brutal life in California ghettos like Compton in Los Angeles and East Bay in Oakland, and in Houston's crime- and drug-infested Fifth Ward. Ice Cube, Too Short, the Geto Boys, and Ice-T described the nightmares of life in the black underclass. Their beats were drawn not from the happy-go-lucky tracks that had characterized the work of early rappers like the Sugar Hill Gang and Kurtis Blow, but from the bass- and drum-filled funk of George Clinton and Rick James. Raps like "Straight Out of Compton," "I'm Your Pusher," and "Mind of a Lunatic" were as bloody and violent as any Clint Eastwood movie. But because they reflected the reality of young black men, they were more disturbing to the American establishment.

Many gangster rappers modeled themselves after characters in the pages of popular paperback novels by Donald Goines and Iceberg Slim. Both writers specialized in seedy tales of the dark side of America's black ghettos. Their books, usually sold in ghetto drugstores, were crammed with racism, sex, violence, drugs, police brutality, and scenes of poverty.

Ice-T (aka Tracy Marrow) was the first California rapper—gangster or otherwise—to challenge East Coast rap. With his straightened hair, light skin, goatee, and ever-present sunglasses, he looked like an Iceberg Slim character come to life. His rap reflected the lifestyles of pimps, stickup men, and other underworld types.

Ice-T also extended his popularity and talent beyond his rap audience. He starred in motion pictures such as *New Jack City*, *Ricochet*, and *Trespass*, playing opposite such heavyweight actors as

Denzel Washington and Wesley Snipes. Ice-T's heavy-metal band, Body Count, generated both cultural breakthroughs and major controversy with songs such as "Cop Killer."

Ice Cube, originally a member of the Compton rap group N.W.A. (Niggas With Attitude), represented the foot patrol of young, uneducated, but streetwise, black men trapped in America's ghettos. Cube rapped about gang warfare, drug dealing, and death: "Another homie got murdered in a shakedown. Now his mother's at the funeral having a nervous breakdown."[17]

Like Ice-T, Ice Cube extended his popularity to the movies. His debut as Doughboy in John Singleton's acclaimed *Boyz N the Hood* was further proof of Cube's reputation as a ghetto realist. Like Ice-T, Cube rapped in what was known as ghettoese, the language of the streets. He endorsed St. Ides, the malt liquor of choice in the ghetto, sold in oversized 40-ounce bottles. When Ice Cube was criticized for promoting an alcoholic beverage to a community that was already plagued by alcohol and substance abuse, he responded by donating the proceeds from his endorsement to community groups.

When others criticized his liberal use of profanity and violence in his music, Cube responded that everything he rapped about was true. The acknowledgments for his second album, *The Predator*, pointed out the anger in Cube's music. Was it part of an entire philosophy and view of history, an in-your-face pose for publicity, or both? The question was part of Cube's intrigue.

Ice Cube wishes to acknowledge white America's continued commitment to the silence and oppression of black men.

Voices and Faces of Rap

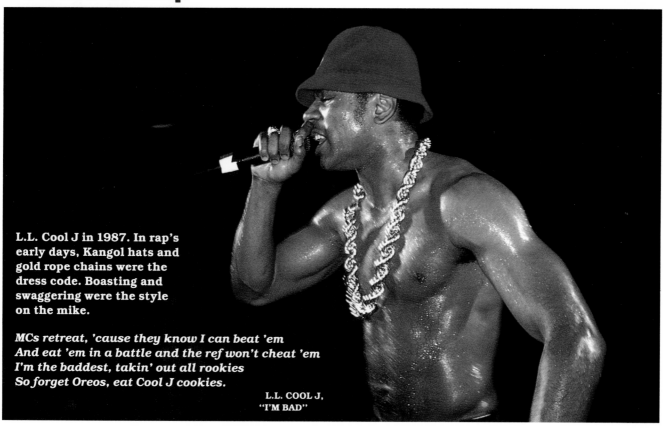

L.L. Cool J in 1987. In rap's early days, Kangol hats and gold rope chains were the dress code. Boasting and swaggering were the style on the mike.

MCs retreat, 'cause they know I can beat 'em
And eat 'em in a battle and the ref won't cheat 'em
I'm the baddest, takin' out all rookies
So forget Oreos, eat Cool J cookies.

L.L. COOL J,
"I'M BAD"

B-boys in the City of Light. Run-D.M.C. performed in Paris in 1987, electrifying audiences and paving the way for the spread of hip-hop worldwide.

Chuck D (*above*) of Public Enemy. The group matched intricate, maze-like rhymes with dense sound-bite collages. A fierce advocate of black pride, it was also wary and self-critical.

As the rhythm designed to bounce
What counts is that the rhymes
Designed to fill your mind
Now that you've realized pride's arrived
We got to pump the stuff to make us tough
From the heart
It's a work of art
To revolutionize make a change nothin's strange
People, people we are the same
No we're not the same
'Cause we don't know the game
What we need is awareness, we can't get careless
You say: What is this?
My beloved let's get down to business
Mental self-defensive fitness.

PUBLIC ENEMY,
"FIGHT THE POWER"

Ice-T freezes for a shot—from the camera. The rapper's exploration—some said exploitation— of tensions between young black men and police made him a target of controversy.

Cops hate kids, kids hate cops
Cops kill kids with warning shots
What is crime and what is not?
What is justice? I think I forgot.
ICE-T,
"SQUEEZE THE TRIGGER"

The Fresh Prince (*right*). To many, his funny, non-controversial raps about dating provided a breath of fresh air.

I took her over town
I wined her and dined her
She asked me did I like her
I said: Well, kinda.
THE FRESH PRINCE,
"GIRLS"

Neither role-model material nor one to mince words, Ice Cube (*left*) sought to expose rather than enlighten in his raps.

It ain't wise to chastise and preach
Just open the eyes of each.
ICE CUBE,
"NIGGA YA LOVE TO HATE"

Digital Underground frontman Humpty Hump. He was a symbol of rap's ability to change, diversify, and even laugh at itself.

Combining sly, sexy, streetwise rhymes with pop hooks was Naughty By Nature. Although it scored mainstream hits with "O.P.P." and "Hip-Hop Hooray," the group declared its commitment to hip-hop first and foremost.

The lamp with a freestyle phantom
Ain't trying to be handsome
Trickin' what you're thinking
'Cause I'm vamping
I live and die for hip-hop
This is hip-hop for today
I give props to hip-hop
So hip-hop hooray.

NAUGHTY BY NATURE,
"HIP-HOP HOORAY"

As rap grew, female rappers came to the forefront. "Latifah's had it up to here," proclaimed Queen Latifah (*above*), perhaps referring to male domination of the mike.

Also committed to hip-hop integrity were white rappers 3rd Bass. Member MC Serch (*above*) rocks the house in this photo.

The rappers of Digable Planets (*right*) reached back to the Beat poetry scene of the 1950s for their image. Their videos showed them in smoky coffee bars reciting to beats laced with the laid-back horns of bebop.

By the early 1990s, rap was open enough to embrace nearly any combination of styles. Speech (*above, front*) and other members of Arrested Development mixed political activism, black Southern culture, and Afro-centrism in their raps.

KRS-One (*above*). He was a symbol of how rap took and transformed such all-American values as the pioneer spirit and being self-made: The New York City streets on which he had been homeless became creative resources on which he built his career as a rapper.

Guru (*above*). His "Jazzmatazz" record took jazz-rap pairing even further. The rapper recorded with a live jazz band that included Branford Marsalis and Donald Byrd.

Realistic, kind of mystic
When I kick this
You should witness the slickness
Of the horn player and the dope
  rhyme sayer
Quite emotional and inspirational
Philosophical and yes very logical.
                    GURU,
                    "LOUNGIN' "

African rappers Zimbabwe Legit were a symbol of rap's return to its place of origin.

Rappers like the Souls of Mischief symbolized rap's ability to move forward, change, and renew itself for the future.

(W.E.B. Du Bois, Marcus Garvey, Stokely Carmichael, H. Rap Brown, the honorable Elijah Muhammed, Minister Farrakhan and all the other brothers that were labeled enemies of the state.)

Ice Cube wishes to acknowledge the failure of the public school system to teach all of its students about the major contributions made by our African-American scientists, inventors, artists, scholars and leaders (with all due respect for your lectures on the planet). Without its role in the conspiracy, the Predator album might not have been made.

Ice Cube wishes to acknowledge America's cops for their systematic and brutal killings of brothers all over the country. (Most of their stories never made it to the camera.) These actions commmited by the police have provided me with some of the material for this album.

To sum it all up, thanks for nothin'! White America needs to thank all black people for still talkin' to them 'cause you know what happens when we stop. You say Ice Cube is a problem—and you're right, he's two people in the same body, one African, one American. I see myself through the eyes of Africa and I will continue to speak as an African. I will become an African American when America gives up oppression of my people. KEEP RAP LEGAL![18]

"You got to give [credit] to a lot of these gangster rappers," Easy Mo Bee stated. "They are talking about hard social issues. They are angry, and this is the only voice they have."[19]

PG RAPPERS   But not all rappers lived their lives on the fringes of urban madness. Rappers like Young M.C. and the Fresh Prince and his turntable counterpart, DJ Jazzy Jeff, represented wholesome but cool young African-American men. In fact, the Fresh Prince and Young M.C. both dropped the kinds of verses that the whole family could enjoy. In his smooth baritone, the Fresh Prince (Will Smith) dropped funny rhymes about double dating, the fantasy of challenging heavyweight boxing champions in the ring, and being trapped in a nightmare with the diabolical Freddie Krueger. "I ain't partners with nobody with nails that long," the Fresh Prince informed the ghoulish star of *Nightmare on Elm Street*.[20]

The duo's work was so clean that it didn't need a parental advisory sticker. "We both have good relationships with our parents," Smith explained. "When Jeff and I started making music, they were always the first to hear it. We wanted to make music that our parents would find acceptable."[21] It was difficult for the pair to become too risqué, especially when they were rehearsing in a kitchen or living-room within earshot of an adult.

Parental considerations aside, Smith also said that in order to get the duo's homemade rap tapes played on the radio in his hometown of Philadelphia, they had to be clean. "At a street level in Philly, you have better access to radio than in any other city," he explained. "It was always easy to get on the rap shows, even if you didn't have a record. A lot of Philly rappers simply didn't curse like the other rappers did, not if they wanted to get on the radio, that is."[22]

The group's hard work paid off. In 1987 they produced rap's first double album, *He's the DJ, I'm the Rapper.* In 1991 they won a

Grammy Award in the newly created rap category for their performance "Summertime," which featured jazz musician Grover Washington, Jr.

Will's comedic flair, which was apparent in his raps, carried over to television. Quincy Jones, the bandleader and record producer who turned his talents to motion pictures and television, chose Smith to play the role of a wayward youth from Philadelphia who is sent to exclusive Bel Air, California, to live with his rich, refined relatives on *The Fresh Prince of Bel Air*. The show became an instant smash. Smith made his dramatic debut in the motion picture *Six Degrees of Separation*, an intense tale of a young black con artist who cheats rich, liberal whites in New York City.

Young M.C., (aka Marvin Young) another Grammy-winning rapper, presented a similar vision of hip-hop. *Stone Cold Rhymin'*, his debut album, gained a foothold in the hip-hop community and in the mainstream. Under Young's interpretation, phrases such as "bust a move," which in its original ghetto meaning referred to sex, became a metaphor for dancing.

Like the Fresh Prince, Young's boasting focused on concerns like afterschool detention and the dating game. An economics major at the University of Southern California, Young stressed that his rap wasn't on the hardcore tip. Still, he held true to the oral tradition and let anyone who doubted his toughness on the microphone know that he wasn't a wimp. On the rhyme "I Come Off," Young delivered a verbal knockout to any old-school rappers who dismissed him as a cream puff, with the technologically correct insult: "You're an eight-track tape and I'm a compact disc."[23]

NATURE OF A SISTER Traditionally, females have been overlooked in the African-American oral tradition. Many critics of the Civil Rights movement, for example, decry the fact that women such as Ella Baker and Fannie Lou Hamer, great activists and speakers in their own right, were infrequently acknowledged for their contributions to the movement in word and deed. However, rap and hip-hop ushered women with microphone skills into the spotlight. Queen Latifah, Salt-N'-Pepa, Roxanne Shanté, Yo Yo, Monie Love, MC Lyte, and others refused relegation to the status of fly-girls, attractive female hangers-on.

The appearance of female rappers was not totally without historical precedent. Poets such as Margaret Walker, Gwendolyn Brooks, Nikki Giovanni, Maya Angelou, and Sonia Sanchez were as noted for their powerful presentations as they were for the strength of their written works.

In the world of rhythm and blues, several female vocalists were noted for their wicked, witty, and captivating monologues. Among them were Millie Jackson, the Queen of Raunch, and lesser-known singers such as Shirley Brown, Barbara Mason, and Betty Wright. These vocalists produced an amusing series of "response" records during the 1970s, in which they "answered" one another's songs with "Woman to Woman" and "From His Woman to You," among others.

In this tradition was Roxanne Shanté (aka Lolita Gooden), hip-hop's female pioneer. In 1984, Shanté cut her first rhyme, "Roxanne's Revenge," in response to "Roxanne, Roxanne" by the group UTFO. In the tune, Shanté waxed profane, independent, and bodacious. She dissed the UTFO crew with the kind of verbal backhand that was usually displayed by male MCs.

Like the music of Betty Wright and Shirley Brown, "Roxanne's Revenge" sparked a slew of other response records from fly-by-night rappers like The Real Roxanne, Roxanne's Doctor, and Roxanne's Psychiatrist. The phenomenon embodied the finest examples of the competitiveness and call and response traditions of black oratory.

On stage Shanté was infamous for putting hecklers, usually smart-mouth men, in their place. In many ways she was the hip-hop daughter of Millie Jackson. Shanté herself flatly admitted: "The only person I admire is Millie Jackson."[24]

In a rap Big Daddy Kane wrote for her called "Have a Nice Day," Shanté launched into a battle cry:

> *'Cause I'm the super female*
> *that's called Shanté*
> *and like Hurricane Annie*
> *I'll blow you away.*
> *Whenever I'm in a battle,*
> *Yo, I don't play.*
> *So you best go about your way*
> *and have a nice day.*[25]

Whereas Shanté was a razor-tongued girl from the projects, Queen Latifah was rap's female cultural ambassador. Latifah is an Arabic name that means "delicate and sensitive." But her rhymes were anything but soft.

From jump street, Latifah (Dana Owens) dropped culture, politics, and nationalism into her rhymes. In "Come into My House," she proclaimed:

The Asiatic black woman hard-core beat drummin',
It's hard to keep a good woman down so I keep comin',
Blow for blow I take and I give some,
Still I rise and I symbolize wisdom.[26]

In interviews Latifah cited her black nationalist upbringing as the inspiration for her work. Her dress was African inspired. Without long hair, light skin, or a slim physique, moreover, Latifah was a departure from the image of the hip-hop fly girl.

Latifah was the *griotte* to Shanté's gossip-monger. Whereas Shanté challenged other female rappers to dis fests, Latifah called for unity and dignity. Latifah was hailed as the female counterpart to KRS-One and Chuck D.

But Latifah's popularity did not end on the microphone. She showed comedic flair in appearances on *The Fresh Prince of Bel Air* and a dramatic presence in the movie *Juice*. She also starred in *Living Single*, a TV situation comedy about four young African-American women living in New York City. In the series Latifah played an ambitious young woman who starts her own magazine. The story reflected Latifah's real life.

Latifah also became a businesswoman. She formed the Flavor Unit Posse, and produced wildly successful hard-core hip-hop acts like BlackSheep, Naughty By Nature, and Apache.

Performers like Salt N' Pepa and Yo Yo added still other dimensions to the female voice in rap. Salt-N'-Pepa, the story goes, met while working part-time in a New York department store. They hit the music scene in 1986 with "Hot, Cool, & Vicious." They developed a rep for being good-natured party girls who politely put guys in their places.

Hailing from the same Los Angeles neighborhood as Ice Cube, Yo Yo (Yolanda Whitaker) represented rap's quintessential ghetto girl, or b-girl. Whereas Salt-N'-Pepa were playful, Yo Yo was a no-nonsense, "around the way girl" who demanded maximum respect, particularly from skeptical rappers of the opposite sex:

> *Here's a piece or chunk of the funkiness.*
> *You can't understand how a sista came up with this*
> *Style that's so wild*
> *And leaves you shiverin' and danglin',*
> *From the way that I be stranglin'.* [27]

Yo Yo projected street smarts and sassiness. Her mother, a community activist in Los Angeles, told one rap journalist that Yo Yo took all of the motherly advice she received during her childhood and put it in her raps.

WHITE RAPPERS As with all forms of African-American music that preceded hip-hop, it was only a matter of time before whites began to rap. The composer George Gershwin used Negro spirituals, blues, and jazz as the basis for his 1935 opera *Porgy and Bess*, which was universally recognized as an "American" masterpiece. Likewise, Elvis Presley became "the King of Rock n' Roll" with an essentially black sound that was calculatedly managed.

The majority of white rappers have met with cold shoulders from the hip-hop community. Many have enjoyed mainstream commercial success. Some, most notably Vanilla Ice, have been one-hit wonders. Others, like 3rd Bass and Young Black Teenagers, have openly acknowledged their indebtedness to the black tradition. They argued that they were legit because they genuinely loved rap, were products of the hip-hop culture, and not out to make a quick buck.

Pop rapper Vanilla Ice (aka Robbie Van Winkle) coasted to popularity on the coattails of Hammer. Ice was originally one of the opening acts on Hammer's 1990 "U Can't Touch This" tour. Hammer had dominated the pop charts for twenty-one weeks with his album, *Please Don't Hurt 'Em, Hammer.* Vanilla Ice's debut, "To the Extreme," knocked Hammer from the number-one spot.

Many believed that Vanilla Ice was a music-industry-manufactured star out to make fast money off black culture. The inevitable comparisons of Ice to Elvis Presley were, however, greatly exaggerated. Unlike Elvis, Ice was a weak imitation of black traditions. Lyrically, his rhymes sounded like a white boy trying to sound "street." He frequently misused hip-hop slang. Rap lovers dismissed his rhymes as "wack," or total garbage. But his artistic offenses were only the tip of the iceberg.

In an insulting attempt to win credibility in both white America and hip-hop circles, Van Winkle presented himself as "hard," lying about his background. In interviews he told of a life of hardship. He claimed that he was a classmate of Luther Campbell — leader of the controversial rap group 2 Live Crew — in a tough Miami high school. He also maintained that he was stabbed in a gang fight. Eventually, a journalist unmasked Van Winkle's fabrications. He turned out to be a middle-class kid from Carrollton, Texas.

Ice became a pariah in the hip-hop community. In their book *Bring on the Noise*, hip-hop critics Havelock Nelson and Michael Gonzales branded him a "bare-faced counterfeit."[28]

After headlining a national tour and recording a live album, suddenly Ice grew quiet. "Let's hope he melted," one hip-hop insider prayed.

The Beastie Boys, on the other hand, were the self-styled Jewish bad boys of rap. This trio of middle-class boys encouraged their fans to party at all costs. The Beasties copied the b-boy swagger in their shows and videos, but that's where their imitations stopped. They appeared onstage in torn jeans and plain T-shirts, the "grunge" uniform of suburban white teens. They sprayed their audiences with beer and rapped about:

> *Beer drinkin', breath stinkin', sniffin' glue,*
> *Belly fillin', always illin', busting caps,*
> *My name's Mike D and I write my own snaps.*[29]

Some hip-hop critics felt that the Beasties mocked black culture. Nonetheless, the Beasties attracted both black and white fans. Their debut album *Licensed to Ill* became the biggest-selling rap album of all time.

Probably the most authentic white rappers to emerge were 3rd Bass, comprised of Pete Nice, MC Serch, and black deejay Richie Rich. Serch and Nice had both grown up in New York City surrounded by black friends and black culture. In fact, being the lone white boys in the chocolate world of rap was second nature to them. As a college student at Columbia University, Nice had the plug pulled on his radio show because he was featuring too much rap.

3rd Bass immediately gained the respect of other rappers—a necessary acknowledgment in the black oral tradition. Their first single, "Product of the Environment," detailed in verse their multicultural upbringing.

> *In the heart of the city, you was born and bred.*
> *You grew up smart or you wound up dead.*
> *Things moved fast but you knew the scoop*
> *And your savior was a rhyme and a beat in a rap group.*[30]

Clearly 3rd Bass was "legit," or closer to the real stuff. They performed in places where the Beastie Boys and Vanilla Ice would never have shown their faces. MC Serch often complained in his raps that 3rd Bass had opened the door for rappers like Vanilla Ice:

> *Hip hop got turned into hit pop.*
> *The second a record was number one on the pop charts.*
> *But don't skip on the heart:*
> *It got its start in the ghetto.*[31]

The group's most popular video, "Pop Goes the Weasel," ended with 3rd Bass beating caricatures of Hammer and Vanilla Ice with mallots.

DANCEHALL RULES In Jamaica, birthplace of DJ Kool Herc, toasting blended with hip-hop. The result was dancehall reggae, a Jamaican rap that bubbled with Caribbean patois, drums, and bass. In many ways rap culture mirrored dancehall culture. The presence of a strong Jamaican community in New York ensured that the two black oral traditions would meet. According to Supercat, one of the leading dancehall deejays:

"Rap and dancehall reggae are similar music. They are the music of the young generations. Both are built on the music of the drum and the bass, the instruments of the rhythm nation. Both come from the same people from the ghetto, from the streets. They're both expressing what they're going through, which are pretty much the same things. The only difference in the two [types of] music is that one of them is plain English, and the other is broken English, which is patois, but it's the same hardcore street stuff."[32]

Artists like Supercat, Shabba Ranks, Daddy Freddy, and Mad Cobra became huge stars with their blend of hip-hop and reggae. Others like the Jamaican-born Heavy D. and Shinehead embraced many traditions. Heavy D. (born Dwight Myers) made a name for himself in rap as "the overweight lover." He extended his rap skills to popular soul music, rapping on the hits of Janet Jackson and her brother, Michael. Heavy also dipped into his Jamaican patois and toasted with Supercat on the dancehall smash, "Big and Ready."

For all of its success, however, dancehall also generated the same kind of criticisms that have plagued hip-hop. Many people saw dancehall as sexist, violent, and vulgar. Shabba Ranks defended his use of "slackness" or profanity, in his immensely popular "Roots and

75

Culture." In one toast, Shabba said that he focused primarily on lyrics about sex because "You got to please John Public when you dealing with the reggae business."[33]

Strong response to antigay comments by Shabba proved that neither dancehall nor rap exists solely as pure entertainment. After he made homophobic remarks on a British talk show, gay rights groups forced Ranks to drop out of a lucrative Bobby Brown tour. If Ranks remained on the bill, the groups promised to protest.

Similarly, young dancehall deejay Buju Banton provoked protests from gays and straights alike with his homophobic tune "Boom Bye Bye." In an unusually violent rap—or gun-lyric, as Jamaicans say—Banton called for the execution of all homosexuals.

COOL LIKE THAT
Back in the days when I was a teenager,
before I had status and before I had a pager,
You could find an abstract listening to hip-hop.
My pops used to say it reminded him of be-bop.
I said, Daddy don't you know that things go in cycles.[34]

By the 1990s, hip-hop's musical and creative base began to move beyond its initial repertoire of James Brown/George Clinton beats and inner city sensibilities. "Alternative" rap, as these newer sounds were called, often incorporated jazz and covered topics as diverse as French philosopher Jean Paul Sartre, homophobia, and life in the rural South. Such expansion broadened rap's audience beyond the streets.

The most popular of the alternative rap groups was Arrested Development. Based in Atlanta, the five-person hip-hop posse created raps that celebrated black womanhood, spirituality, and the beauty of life beyond America's tense inner cities and plastic suburbs: "Dig your hands in the dirt, Children play with earth."[35]

"There are a lot of people who look up to rappers," Speech, the leader of Arrested Development, told *DJ Times* magazine. "I want people to be aware that sometimes what artists are saying isn't always right. I guess I'm giving another perspective."[36]

While the group's rap didn't pack the hard-core rhymes of groups like Public Enemy, they won credibility with hip-hop fans and newcomers alike. "They don't sound like the usual rap group," *The Wall Street Journal* sniffed. "[The band's] favorite 'F' word is freedom."[37] In addition to performing with live musicians, Arrested Development incorporated banjos, harmonicas, and other instruments not traditionally used in hip-hop.

Several musicians and rappers explored the common ground between jazz and hip-hop. The most notable groups were Freestyle Fellowship, Digable Planets, saxophonist Greg Osby, and the rappers Gang Starr, based in Brooklyn, New York. Many jazz musicians noted that hip-hop, like jazz, was created from an outcast culture. When A Tribe Called Quest teamed with great jazz bassist Ron Carter to produce their 1991 album *The Low End Theory*, the results were ear-catching. They also opened up a whole new world of sampling. Artists like Tribe, Gang Starr, and Digable Planets delved into the works of saxophonists Eddie Harris and Sonny Rollins, organist Grant Green, and the Jazz Crusaders.

In 1993 saxophonist Greg Osby released a hip-hop album *3-D Lifestyles* with Philadelphia-based 100X. The album was released on Blue Note records, the premiere straight-ahead jazz label in the United States.

On the opening credits of the album *Jazzmatazz*, Guru (Gifted Unlimited Rhymes Universal) of Gang Starr laid his vision cards on the table as jazz trumpeter Donald Byrd played a bluesy melody in the background:

Welcome to Jazzmatazz, an experimental fusion of hip-hop and live jazz. Now I've always thought of doing something like this, but I didn't want to do it unless it was gonna be done right, know what I'm saying? Rap music is real. It's musical cultural expression based on reality, and at the same time jazz is real, based on reality. So I want to let you know that it was indeed a blessing to work on such a project with so many amazing people.[38]

Many rappers and musicians saw rap as an art form that would only continue to evolve. To them, the days of the simple MC rhymes at the playground were long gone. As more musicians explored hip-hop, the marriage between rhyme, rhythm, and music became even stronger. Although rap's musical base was expanding, it remained an art form dominated by the griot tradition.

Technology

ROOTS,

FREE SPEECH and,

Culture,

Chapter Five

Paris is my name, I don't sleep,

I drop science and keep the peace,

Here to bust this for better justice,

Another dope Scarface release.

This is a serious style for the gifted,

Pro-Black radical raps upliftin',

Still growin', the powers so strong,

You can't stop it now.

PARIS
"BREAK THE GRIP OF SHAME"[1]

Probably one
of the most
amazing aspects

of the rap music explosion was that it managed to sell to millions of fans with relatively little radio play for a long time. In this respect, rap's commercial growth continued the "word of mouth" tradition that had given birth to it.

Radio initially shied away from rap on the grounds that it would not appeal to advertisers. Instead, the "softer" sounds of singers like Michael Jackson, Whitney Houston, and Luther Vandross were widely played. To many, however, "softer" meant less black.

**OUT OF THE
'HOOD AND BACK**

But when rap did break into radio, and the rest of the media, it challenged America's notions about what it meant to be a star.

For all their popularity, rappers essentially remained connected to their communities or, in rap terms, from the 'hood. Queen Latifah and Big Daddy Kane (Kane stands for King Asiatic Nobody's Equal) sold millions of albums and still acted like ordinary people. Unlike many African-American pop musicians, most rappers expressed no desire to cross over to fame in mainstream—which to some meant white—America. Nor did they attempt to imitate mainstream codes of dress and demeanor once they became successful.

An integral part of maintaining flavor, or credibility, in hip-hop was simply being yourself. "It's important for people in my neighborhood [the Bedford-Stuyvesant area of Brooklyn, New York] to see that I can make it and not give up being a black man," observed Easy Mo Bee. "Young brothers around my way might sell drugs. They ain't never been too ambitious or prompted to do anything positive. I can charge them up. When they hear Miles [Davis] or Big Daddy Kane or see my face in the media, they know I'm from the neighborhood. The fellas can look at me and be influenced."[2]

Once a rapper lost contact with "the streets," his or her career was all but over. The eccentric behavior of pop stars like Madonna, Michael Jackson, or Prince didn't play to many in the hip-hop community. Such behavior would be dismissed as "wack" or totally out of line with the hip-hop community, and definitely hurt a rapper's all-important reputation.

According to Tajai of the Souls of Mischief: "If you stray from the foundation, you're going to crumble. People aren't going to give you any type of credibility. Maybe the mainstream, who's not really down with hip-hop and haven't grown with it since it started, and can't understand it, they might like you, but people who understand the roots of hip hop will totally cut you off."[3]

In the 1992 hit "No Nose Job," Digital Underground offered a biting criticism of stars who "sell out" once they cross over to a wider audience. Led by the social commentator and group funnyman Humpty Hump, the rap made thinly veiled references to the physical appearance of Michael Jackson, who has been frequently accused of changing his features through cosmetic surgery to make himself more appealing to mainstream audiences.

> Yo, Humpty, now that your records are selling,
> Ain't it about time for you to start bailing out
> of the race and community that you come from?
> Yo, your face has got to change, son.[4]

82

In the rap, Humpty is confronted by a plastic surgeon, who tells him that cosmetic surgery is the only way he will become a huge star. They argue. The rap, set to a George Clinton-like groove, ends with Humpty escaping from the doctor's office, nose intact, and bidding his fans "peace and Humptiness forever."

By remaining ethnic and, to some, even raw, deejays and MCs became living proof that being successful was possible without betraying one's roots or race. This belief would be a fundamental element of hip-hop culture. Rappers provided hope to millions of fans who were otherwise trapped in bleak existences, who had to search far beyond the government, the educational system, and the media for role models they could relate to. Rappers' frequent use of passwords for ambition — "getting paid" or "living large" — exhorted listeners to rise above their surroundings. Posses parading through the 'hood in the latest styles showed that young African Americans shared the material aspirations of all Americans, but realized them on their terms.

Mainstream publications such as *The Wall Street Journal* and *Black Enterprise* magazine noted that hip-hop mogul Russell Simmons built a $35-million-a-year-empire without ever wearing a suit and tie. Simmons sported a shaved head and favored "phat," or cool, gear like hooded sweatshirts, jeans, and lumberjack boots. "Black families are traditionally taught how to go to school, get an education and then, do your thing. But a lot of black businessmen come from street culture and an attitude that says, start your own, do your own. It's counterculture," Simmons said.[5]

To some, however, this open celebration of blackness and self-determination was threatening. And where it was pronounced enough, it attracted controversy. In his essay "Rap Music as American History," Jefferson Morley noted:

> The racial implications of rap offer an alternative to the liberal ideal of integrationism and the conservative idea of a 'colorblind' society. Rap's mass success is not based on blacks accepting white middle-class values, or on the allegedly declining significance of race in American culture . . . but on an ideal at once more realistic and more radical: that in America blacks and whites alike will celebrate black values, instead of expecting blacks to accept white values.[6]

DON'T BELIEVE THE HYPE? Does speaking out always mean not selling out—or is there a point at which speaking out can offend others unnecessarily or even cause harm? This question became all-important for rap in 1990 when the group 2 Live Crew was charged with obscenity. On June 8, a Florida record store owner was arrested for selling the group's album *As Nasty As They Wanna Be.* Two days later, the group was arrested after a live performance at a Florida club. The charges in both cases stemmed from the lyrics in the group's raps: According to local law enforcement officials, their use of profanity and sexually explicit content violated ordinances against obscene speech.

The arrests and attempts to prevent the sale of the albums in Florida and elsewhere sparked heated debate. Noted scholar Dr. Henry Louis Gates, Jr., who served as an expert witness on black oratory in the 2 Live Crew case, argued that the black oral tradition had always encompassed boasting and sexual exaggerations. The raps were not meant to be taken literally. Someone who was ignorant of the black oral tradition, therefore, was in no position to pass judgment on 2 Live Crew.

Gates pointed out that the raps of 2 Live Crew were no different from the routines of chitlin' circuit comedians such as Redd Foxx and Rudy Ray Moore. "2 Live Crew must be interpreted within the context of black culture generally."[7]

Not everyone agreed. Many African Americans argued that to mention the locker-room rantings of 2 Live Crew's Luther Campbell in the same breath as the spellbinding oratory of Martin Luther King was cultural treason. The case galvanized the music industry. While many artists admitted that 2 Live Crew's brand of rap might be "garbage," they felt the group's right to free speech was protected by the Constitution.

The record store owner was convicted, but the group won its case. Neither ruling, however, ended the controversy over how far rappers could or couldn't go in expressing themselves in their raps.

One organization, the Parents Music Resource Center (PMRC), felt that the content of some contemporary music, particularly rap and heavy metal, needed monitoring. In 1985, Tipper Gore, wife of Clinton Administration vice president Al Gore, founded PMRC with several other wives of politicians. According to the organization, PMRC's purpose was to promote responsibility and self-restraint in the record industry. Gore and others were disturbed by the violence, racism, brutality toward women, and glamorization of drugs and alcohol in this type of music.

PMRC proposed a record rating system to the Recording Industry Association of America, the independent agency that regulates the music industry. Ratings would be administered by a review board. However, as in the 2 Live Crew case, it became clear that interpretation of an artist's lyrics was subject to all kinds of bias. This was especially the case for many in the rap community. Rappers felt that their speech was a part of their culture, and those who didn't understand the culture or lifestyle weren't fit to judge the speech.

Eventually a compromise was reached. PMRC advocated the placement of a sticker warning of "Explicit Lyrics" and calling for a "Parental Advisory" on all albums and CDs that might contain "objectionable" subject matter.

Ice-T, one of the rappers criticized by PMRC, responded with his pro-First Amendment rap, "Freedom of Speech," addressing Tipper Gore as "Tip":

> *The Constitution says we all got a right to speak.*
> *Say what we want, Tip, your argument is weak.*
> *Censor records, TV, school books, too?*
> *And who decides what's right to hear, you?*
> *PMRC this is where the witchhunt starts.*[8]

POLICE AND POSSES The "hardest" raps with the greatest credibility in African-American communities maintained a topicality the significance of which, many believed, eluded listeners from more privileged backgrounds or from different ethnic groups. Police brutality, for example, has been a centuries-old issue in the African-American community. Perhaps one of the most eloquent African-American perspectives on why police invoke suspicion and resentment among blacks—particularly urban black males—was offered by the writer James Baldwin. Baldwin observed of the police presence in Harlem, New York City, during the 1950s:

[T]he only way to police a ghetto is to be oppressive. None of the Police Commissioner's men, even with the best will in the world, have any way of understanding the lives led by the people, as they swagger about in twos and threes controlling. Their very presence is an insult, and it would be, even if they spent their entire day feeding gumdrops to children. They represent the force of the white world, and that world's criminal profit and ease, to keep the black man corralled up here, in his place. . . .

[The policeman in Harlem] has never, himself, done anything for which to be hated—which of us has?—and yet he is facing, daily and nightly, people who would gladly see him dead, and he knows it. There is no way for him not to know it: There are few things under heaven more unnerving than the silent, accumulating hatred and contempt of a people. He moves through Harlem, therefore, like an occupying soldier in a bitterly hostile country, which is . . . the reason he walks in twos and threes.[9]

Perhaps more than any other contemporary art form, rap confronted, some forty years after Baldwin's statement, this ongoing struggle between the black community and the police. Not surprisingly, it invited controversy. Ice-T's 1991 release "Cop Killer," a violent monologue from the point of view of a murderer of law enforcement officials, was released through his heavy-metal band Body Count. Nonetheless, rap took heat for the song. Authorities across the country (including President George Bush and Vice President Dan Quayle) condemned the song. Others called for a boycott of Ice-T's record label, Time Warner, and stores carrying the album. Some

1,400 record stores around the country pulled the record from their shelves. When the smoke finally cleared, Ice-T withdrew the cut from the album.

Freedom of speech debates ensued. Many wondered if Ice-T, a former stick-up man and gang member, was advocating lawlessness or violence. Others wondered: Was he speaking in the tradition of the griots about the everyday experiences of his culture, and simply doing so in exaggerated terms?

Dancehall artist Super Cat, who applauded the outspokenness of rappers like Ice-T and Ice Cube, observed that America was hypocritical, and didn't understand the place of boasting in black oratory. "Some people say that rap music is the devil's music. They can say what they want to say. There is violence in every aspect of what I see going on in America. If you go to the movies to see a movie by Sylvester Stallone or Clint Eastwood, these guys don't smile throughout the entire movie. They are blowing people away. I don't see how a guy on the stage just talking, with no picture, could be more violent than a movie. We didn't create this problem, so they cannot just blame the youth for this."

"Ice-T is just playing a tough character, just like a movie star," Cat continued. "He doesn't literally mean 'Go out there and kill cop' because if he meant that, he himself would be out there doing that."

Moreover, Cat pointed out, rap fans fully understand the difference between talk and action. "There's no cop out there getting shot because Ice-T says shoot the cop."[10]

None of Ice-T's critics were able to point to any instances where the tune had provoked citizen violence against police. Nonetheless, it was blasted by many, among them California's Attorney General Daniel E. Lungren, as "a bold incitement to kill."[11]

Some took widespread criticism of Ice-T as evidence that blacks who expressed ugly or violent thoughts received harsher treatment than whites who did the same. Such inequality, these people pointed out, only moved blacks to reject whites more. According to Dr. Cornell West: "As long as double standards and differential treatment abound—as long as the rap performer Ice-T is harshly condemned while former Los Angeles Police Chief Daryl F. Gates's anti-black comments are received in polite silence . . . black nationalism will thrive."[12] (Daryl Gates was the outspoken chief of the Los Angeles Police Department at the time of the Rodney King incident.)

Privately, many rappers feared that the "Cop Killer" controversy would open a Pandora's box on their freedom of expression. "It's a shame that rap had to take the fall for something Ice-T did with a metal band," commented one rapper who wished to remain anonymous. "The only thing that's going to stick is that he's a rap artist."

Such sentiments proved prophetic. In the aftermath of the "Cop Killer" controversy, several record labels began to closely monitor the lyrical content of rap albums. Time Warner rejected Ice-T's next album *Home Invasion* and released him from his contract. The releases of several rap albums were delayed while record company executives "negotiated" the contents with artists. Paris, a member of the Nation of Islam and a follower of the Black Panther party, generated widespread attention when he refused to remove the anti-George Bush rap "Bush Killa" from his second album. In the rap, Paris daydreams of assassinating the former president.

Paris had long maintained that the true intent of would-be censors was not to silence sexually explicit and exaggeratedly violent raps of 2 Live Crew or Too Short. Such forces, he argued, were much more concerned with silencing militant and overtly political rap. "The censorship that has been directed towards rap music thus far is really a smokescreen to get to the artists who truly have something to say," he said. "I don't promote mindless violence, glorify the drug trade, misogyny [hatred of women] or racial intolerance. People who do [that kind of] negative rap are very hard to defend. It's quite easy to defend what I'm talking about. This system has never been designed for people of color, and by exposing the ills of this society, a lot of rap is blowing the whistle on the oppressive factors in the way we live. Artists like myself have an agenda that the people who control this country may view as threatening."[13]

Tommy Boy, Paris's record company, refused to issue the album. After much legal wrangling, Paris secured a substantial settlement from the company and released the album, in its entirety, on his own label, Scarface Records.

To many, Paris obviously had a point. Beyond the relatively apolitical obscenity of 2 Live Crew lay more fundamental issues. Every time a rapper like 2 Live Crew's Luther Campbell was accused of lewdness, there were other rappers—such as Paris, P.E., N.W.A., and Ice Cube—who were accused of promoting unrest with their blistering raps about sensitive topics: relationships between African Americans and other ethnic groups such as Jews, Koreans, and law enforcement officials as well as AIDS and homosexuality.

RAP AND THE WHITE HOUSE By 1992, rap had become an issue in the presidential campaign. Following the acquittal of four Los Angeles police officers in the criminal trial for the beating of black motorist Rodney King, the city's black and Latino ghettos burst into violence. Immediately media attention focused on rappers. Even before the King incident, rappers from P.E. to N.W.A. had foretold large-scale urban unrest that would be provoked by police brutality. In the song "Burn Hollywood Burn," from Public Enemy's 1990 release *Fear of a Black Planet*, Chuck D warned:

Burn Hollywood burn. I smell a riot
Goin' on, first they're guilty now they're gone.

He was joined on the same song by Ice Cube, whose rap seemed to predict with disturbing accuracy the King beating and its violent aftermath:

Roamin' through Hollywood late at night,
Red and blue lights what a common sight,
Pulled to the curb gettin' played like a sucker,
Don't fight the power [sound of gunfire] the m———f———.[14]

Some authorities openly wondered if rap music itself had not provoked the violence. Rappers responded that authorities, perhaps, should listen to rap. "People listen to our music and realize what we're talking about is right outside their front door," said MC Ren (aka Lorenzo Patterson) of N.W.A. "Stuff we was [saying] on records we been saying since 1987 and 1988, telling about police brutality, but nobody wanted to listen."[15]

Bill Clinton, the democratic presidential contender, blasted P.E. protegé Sister Souljah (aka Lisa Williamson) for comments she made about the riots in the *Washington Post*.[16]

Clinton compared Souljah, a self-proclaimed "raptivist," to David Duke, a former Klansman who ran for governor of Louisiana in

91

1991 on a platform of what many perceived as thinly disguised racist ideas. An angry Souljah responded that Clinton had taken her remarks out of context. She accused him of attacking her in order to show white voters he could control unrest in the inner cities.

Still, a measure of rap's influence on American culture was evident in the 1993 inauguration of President Bill Clinton. At the Lincoln Memorial, L.L. Cool J upstaged pop stars like Michael Jackson and Diana Ross when he exhorted well-wishers to say "ho" and party with "Big Bill and Hillary."

At separate festivities, First Daughter Chelsea Clinton sang along with Salt-N'-Pepa during the trio's performance of the anti-AIDS rap "Let's Talk About AIDS."

SAMPLING   Regardless of legalities or taboos, rappers refused to be silenced.

That was the case, at least, except where the unique rap technology of assembling songs from pieces of other songs—sampling—was concerned. Once again, the controversy was linked to cultural issues. In the black oral tradition that gave rise to rap, expressions and ideas were always communal property. Rarely was individual ownership declared of words or music. James Brown could holler "Good God!" in the heat of performance and C.L. Franklin could proclaim the same words during a sermon. When rappers sampled the songs of James Brown and others they were merely continuing a time-honored tradition.

Or were they? Even in rap's early days, sampling attracted controversy. Some musicians labeled sampling as theft. Acts like Sugar Hill Gang took entire songs and simply placed rap lyrics on top of existing rhythms and melodies. "Rapper's Delight," for example, was set to the music of the disco megahit "Good Times," by Chic. The group sued Sugar Hill Gang for infringement of copyright and was awarded $500,000.

Still, hip-hop journalist Greg Tate praised sampling: "Making old records talk via scratching or sampling is fundamental to hip-hop." In his review of the P.E. album *It Takes a Nation of Millions to Hold Us Back*, Tate acknowledged the crew's sampling genius: "P.E. has evolved a songcraft from chipped flecks of near-forgotten soul gold. On *Nation* a guitar vamp from Funkadelic, a moan from Sly, a growl abducted from Bobby Byrd aren't just rhythmically spliced in but melodically sequenced into colorful narratives."[17]

But the hip-hop community was by no means in unanimous agreement over sampling. In 1990 Hammer's "U Can't Touch This" received the Grammy for best rhythm and blues performance. Punk-funk rocker Rick James, whose song "Super Freak" was sampled for the tune, also received a Grammy. Still, rappers accused Hammer of "biting" James's song—that is, copycatting his work.

In the days when rap was run by small record companies, no one paid attention to the pieces of music rappers used. If the groove of the music matched that of the rapper, that was all that mattered. "Nobody knew and nobody cared," an entertainment attorney commented.

By 1989 things had changed. Rap's audience had widened and artists demanded payment when portions of their music were sampled. Several rappers were sued for failure to obtain permission and copyright clearance to use certain musical segments. The biggest case involved Biz Markie. In 1990 a judge ruled that Biz had sampled

"Alone Again, Naturally," a song by English pop singer Gilbert O'Sullivan, without permission. As a condition of settlement, the court ordered Biz Markie's company to withdraw his album from the market.

In the aftermath of the Biz decision, record companies established strict guidelines for sampling. Suddenly a new set of lawyers became involved in rap. Albums that required too many clearances were delayed in limbo or "sample hell." Biz's next album, released three years later, was good-naturedly entitled *All Samples Cleared*.

But were such legal restrictions a form of censorship? "Sampling is central . . . to rap," wrote *New York Times* reporter Sheila Rule. She explained that rap originated in poor neighborhoods where "borrowing bits of many songs to build a piece of music began as a necessity and evolved into something of an art form."[18] Rap had put an interesting spin on the issue of free speech. Were people free — in the literal sense — to use the speech and music of others?

Many artists willingly granted rappers the right to use their songs — for a fee. Often deals were cut. When Naughty by Nature sampled the Jackson Five hit "A.B.C." for their 1991 smash "O.P.P.," they gave co-writing credits to the original composers. That meant the orignal writers shared a percentage of the profits from record sales with the rappers. War, a major Latin jazz funk band of the 1970s, had been sampled by many rappers. In 1992 the group, off the music scene for many years, released *Rap Declares War*, a collection of the band's songs that rappers had sampled. Brand Nubian, Ice-T, Too Short, and Nice and Smooth were among the rappers represented on the album. The release showed that rap could compromise and continue to grow.

chapter SIX

Stylin' and Profilin'

Alright, stop what you're doing,
Cause I'm about to ruin
the image and style that you're used to.

I look funny, but yo,
I'm making money,
So I hope you're ready for me.

And all the rappers in the Top 10
please allow me to bump thee.

I'm stepping tall, ya'll,
and just like Humpty Dumpty
You're gonna fall
when the stereos pump me.

I'm sick with this
Straight Gangster Mack.

DIGITAL UNDERGROUND
"THE HUMPTY DANCE"[1]

And rap did grow.

By the early 1990s, not only had rap's influence shown itself in nearly every other form of popular music, but it was everywhere in the media. The days when MCs hawked homemade cassettes at basement parties and on playgrounds were over. The art form became a multimillion dollar industry that encompassed music, videos, and fashion. *Black Enterprise* magazine estimated that in 1992 rap music alone generated $400 million in sales.

BACK ON THE BLOCK In 1990 producer Quincy Jones helped to put rap in a bold new musical context with his *Back on the Block* album. Jones had produced a trio of best-selling albums for Michael Jackson in the 1980s: *Off the Wall, Bad,* and *Thriller,* which became the best-selling album of all time. Jones was ready to record new material. He wanted to produce an album that would encompass the broad spectrum of African-American music.

Jones's children had been rap fans for years, and he was already open to the music. When he met rappers like L.L. Cool J and Run D.M.C., Jones immediately noted the similarities between them and the be-bop jazz musicians with whom he had worked decades before. He commended rappers for their way with words, their dress, and their value system—all of which ignored convention. He also educated rappers to the fact that they were part of a longstanding cultural and musical legacy. Jones called rap "the most passionate music in America," in *Listen Up,* a documentary of his life. "The words slap people in the face with vivid, graphic reality."[2]

Jones secured the services of Big Daddy Kane, Ice-T, Melle Mel, and Kool Moe Dee for his album. The rappers worked alongside jazz greats like guitarist George Benson, Dizzy Gillespie, Miles Davis, and a promising young pop singer named Tevin Campbell.

The album kicked off with Jones reciting a rap written by his son, Quincy Jones III, and Big Daddy Kane:

'Cause I been away for a long long time,
now I'm not only back, but I'm here to rhyme.
So bust the mood as I include
that I'm back on the block
portraying the dude.

The elder Jones's MC-ing skills certainly posed no threat to the real rappers, but his gesture provided a strong endorsement for rap. Throughout the album the quartet of rappers, in the lyrics of Kane, "let poetry bloom to who it may concern or consume."[3]

The most interesting songs on the album showcased the rappers with jazz giants and a choir. On the title track, Kane, Melle Mel, Kool Moe Dee, and Ice-T took turns busting rhymes while Tevin Campbell sang in Swahili and English about an African dude named Stoki who loved teasing girls.

Meanwhile, other nonrap artists were featuring rappers on their songs with great results. Chaka Khan scored a massive hit with a Prince tune, "I Feel for You," which featured Melle Mel detailing his infatuation with the vocalist. Shabba Ranks, reggae dancehall's top toaster, teamed with reggae crooner Maxi Priest for the explosive "House Call." An ode to a lover's desire, "House Call" zoomed straight to the top of the charts. The interplay between Priest and Ranks was seamless. Whereas their American cousins were content to cut vocals and rap tracks separately, the Jamaicans grooved together. In heavy Jamaican patois, Shabba hypnotically chanted:

> *Me 'ave the remedy for yer heart*
> *Me 'ave the remedy for yer brain.*[4]

Priest's ad lib: "These are your doctors / Maxi Priest and Shabba, Shabba, Shabba" would be sampled by countless hip-hop and dancehall deejays.

In still other blurrings of rap's boundaries, several gospel groups incorporated Christian-oriented raps into their music. The Winans, America's leading gospel group, employed the services of Teddy Riley, the king of New Jack Swing and producer of Heavy D., Big Daddy Kane, Kool Moe Dee, and Wrecx N' Effect, and cut the tune "It's Time (To Make a Change)." The groove opened with Riley prophesying:

> *Well it's time to make that change,*
> *People of the world today are fading.*
> *All of us have our ups and downs,*
> *Better think about it or you wouldn't be around.*
> *What we need is a little bit of love*
> *Sent by one straight from heaven up above.*
> *Take it from T:*
> *It's simple and plain.*
> *This ain't no game,*
> *You know what I'm saying?*[5]

Riley was then joined by the robust harmonies of the Winan brothers who, like Aretha Franklin, Jesse Jackson, and others, grew up in the black church.

Some conservative elements of the gospel music community blasted the song as worldly, but it was still a huge hit. The Winans defended their hip-hop choice by arguing that one must spread the Good News in manners by which it reaches people. And if that means meeting those in need of deliverance on the dance floor, so be it.

"Those [critics in the church] are people who just look at the lifestyle of rappers and not what the art form is," declared popular Christian rapper Mike E. "Rapping is just like talking. You can talk in secular language, or you can speak in the language of Christians."

Mike E., a native of Detroit who grew up in a Pentecostal church pastored by his father, prided himself on producing raps that are just as "hard" as those of Ice Cube or Public Enemy. "Some people think that people who are from religious backgrounds are sheltered from the woes of life," he noted, "but we're not. I faced the same problems that Ice Cube and Ice-T faced. I've been pulled over by the same police. Life is not always sunshine, flowers, and rainbows. Rap deals with real-life situations, and a lot of people, both inside and outside of the church, simply don't want to hear about it."[6]

Christ, Mike adds, was the ultimate rebel. "During his tenure on earth, Jesus hung out in the streets. He wasn't at shrines or temples. He was in the ghettos."

Mike readily acknowledged that music and oratory were a part of his heritage. "My dad's a minister, and I come from a long line of preachers. So, I figure that my rapping is just the minister in me coming out. I just preach a bit more rhythmically [than my fore-bearers]."[7]

Up every morning and you gotta meet the man.
Two hundred years later and you still don't understand
How you work like a slave puttin' in the hours,
Dazed and amazed that they still got the power.
Forty acres and a mule was the promise that they gave us.
Today forty hours and a tool is how they slave us.
Study the word and let it hide your heart.
That'll be the thing that'll set you apart.[8]

RAP ON THE AIRWAVES Not only had rap spilled over into other forms of music, but it proved itself immensely adaptable to other media. The expansion of cable TV and the launching of MTV ushered in the popularity of short-form videos, which quickly became another tool for promoting popular music. The ensuing wedding of the African-American oral tradition and the video age was a logical one. Rappers like Kid 'N Play, Hammer, and P.E. were picture-perfect for music videos. With his baggy Ali Baba pants and frantic dancing, Hammer was perhaps more popular for his look than he was for his raps. Similarly, Play's hair, standing tall like a woolly Sears Tower, was attention-grabbing. (Hammer and Kid 'N Play were featured in Saturday morning cartoon shows.) Also photogenic were the gigantic stopwatch and oversized sunshades that P.E. rapper Flavor Flav sported.

In 1988 MTV introduced the rap show *Yo, MTV Raps!* The program was hosted by a trio of fly guys: artist and hip-hop celebrity Fab 5 Freddy, who was immortalized by Blondie in the rap hit "Rapture," Dr. Dre, and Ed Lover, who went on to star in hip-hop's first whodunnit flick, *Who's the Man?*. Within weeks the program was the most popular on the twenty-four-hour music channel's lineup. *Yo MTV Raps!* managed to bring hip-hop culture to America on a weekly basis.

Two black television shows with mass appeal, *The Arsenio Hall Show* and *In Living Color*, also gave rap the kind of exposure that it did not get on traditional prime-time television. Hall gave America a funky alternative to the staid humor of late-night TV king Johnny Carson. The show's inclusion of hip-hop artists of every persuasion from Ice-T to Kid N' Play prompted Carson and his successor Jay Leno to diversify their roster of guests. In addition to having rappers perform on his show, Hall also interviewed them.

In Living Color, a black-oriented comedy show that was carried by the ground-breaking Fox Broadcasting Company, capitalized on hip-hop sensibilities. The show's dance company, the Fly Girls, were featured every week in a hip-hop dance segment. The show's weekly finale showcased America's hottest rappers performing songs that usually weren't played on radio. Profanities were beeped out of the performance, but that was the extent of censorship. As the program's closing credits rolled, the show's entire cast boogied in the background as their rap guests performed.

Gradually rap was moving beyond its origins in the 'hood and into mainstream America. The Reverend Jesse Jackson, a nonrapper in the musical sense, gave rap a high five when he hosted the comedy show *Saturday Night Live* in 1984. In one of the skits, Jackson concluded a satirical newscast with a rap and a beat box.

Beyond its visual compatibility with video, rap proved popular on the large screen. Early efforts to present rap in movies such as *Beat Street* and *Krush Groove* failed to portray hip-hop culture credibly. However, later films like Spike Lee's *Do the Right Thing*, Ernest Dickerson's *Juice*, and John Singleton's *Boyz N the Hood* used rap and clearly reflected the lifestyle of young blacks living in American cities. When presented in straight dramas, rappers like Ice-T, Ice Cube, and 2 Pac—who played a psychotic gunslinging youth in *Juice*—came across strong. Meanwhile, in comedy, Kid 'N Play ruled the silver screen with *House Party* and *House Party II*.

Robert Townsend, the director of films such as *Hollywood Shuffle* and *Five Heart Beats*, said that rap lends itself to cinema. "The rap artists are very comfortable with the camera," Townsend noted. "It's the natural transition from one medium to the next. With music videos you have to act. You've got to be able to punch the lyrics through that television. Rappers are used to doing that."

Meteor Man, Townsend's 1993 urban fairy tale, featured rappers Naughty By Nature and Cypress Hill. "I needed rappers in my movie, because they're the heroes that kids look up to these days," Townsend said. "Rappers are the true prophets of today. They're the ones who are really saying what's going on in this country."[9]

While preserving its lifeline to black culture, rap managed to also tie into mainstream America. But the United States wasn't the only country in which modern-day griots were speaking out.

CHAPTER SEVEN

GLOBAL RAP

Hip-Hop Rules

Rules

en
fashion
or not to
would rather
portin' beads and a
dallion on your chest, but d
ion. To me, Afrocentricity is kinda spiritual. Some M
in your heart? Many MCs I see are hypocritical. Now s
it ian. off the bandwagon and pull the cart.
cart. 'Cause in the past, rappers were into braggin'. Me
pirtual. But at this time, Africa's the center of attraction. Jum
cal. Everyone is cashin' in on the fashion. To me, Afrocentricity is
aggin. To bead or not to bead, that is what I'm askin'. Many MCs I s
ter of attraction. Some MCs would rather be Italian. 'Cause in the past,
n the fashion: Now sportin' beads and a black medallion. But at this time,
t I'm askin'. Medallion on your chest, but do you feel it in your heart? To me,
medallion. Jump off the bandwagon and pull the cart. Everyone is cashin' in
To me, Afrocentricity is kinda spiritual. Many MCs see are hypocritical. 'Caus
e in the past, rappers were into b rag
this time. Africa's the center of at But at
traction. Everyone is cashin' in
on the fashion: To bead or not
to bead, that is what I'm askin'. S
ome MCs would rather be Ita
lian. Now sportin' beads an
d a black medallion. Me
dallion on your che
st, but do
you

ZIMBABWE LEGIT
"TO BEAD OR NOT TO BEAD"[1]

Rap's influence has extended

Rap's influence has extended not only far beyond its origins in African-American ghettos but beyond the United States itself. It is a global phenomenon. As one journalist put it, rap has "left its fingerprints all over mainstream popular music," around the world.[2]

In the beginning, foreign rappers imitated Americans like L.L. Cool J, Chuck D, and Salt-N'-Pepa. Soon, however, the imitation gave way to rap in native tongues, and reflected particular regional concerns. Rap, no matter where it was, almost always reflected the spirit of urban youth.

EUROPE In 1982, Afrika Bambaataa and Fab 5 Freddy headlined the first rap tours to Europe. They made a lasting impression in London, and particularly in Paris. Soon French intellectuals and music lovers alike didn't refer to rap music, but rather to *le mouvement rap*, the rap movement. The French embraced rap as a political expression, an art form, and a way of life. Rap was encouraged through exhibitions, scholarships, and grants for study, and France's minister of culture stated that it was his obligation to be committed "to a movement so filled with life."[3]

As in other countries, the first French rappers merely copied Americans. Then gradually the rappers started to talk about their lives in France. "We were nowhere until people could learn to rap in French and speak about French topics," said French rap radio show host, Oliver Cachin.[4]

Paris has always embraced the creations of African-American culture like the blues and jazz. Paris also has had a strong African, Arab, and Caribbean immigrant population. The result of this cultural blend was a new oral tradition. Parisian rap combined elements of the oral traditions of Africa, America, and Europe. By the 1990s the city boasted at least ten major rap groups. One of the country's most popular radio shows was *Rapline*.

Supreme N.T.M. became known as the French Public Enemy. They used the hard-core street language of many of the tough neighborhoods of Paris. The most popular French rap artist of the early 1990s was the Senegal-born MC Solaar. In 1992 Solaar received the coveted Victorie de La Musique (the equivalent of a Grammy) for Best Artist. In 1993, Solaar appeared on the American-produced album *Jazzmatazz*, an ambitious pairing of hip-hop and jazz, in a duet with American MC Guru, "Le Bien, Le Mal" ("The Good and the Bad"). One American reviewer noted that Solaar's voice and microphone were "so spellbinding, it almost ceases to matter whether or not you understand the words he's speaking. His vibe is clear."[5]

Solaar's thick, clear French literally jumped out of the recording. French never sounded funkier. "His lyrics, filled with humor, intelligence, and metaphors, push the poetic potential of the French language," reviewer David Sinclair noted.[6]

A *New York Times* reviewer added: "If hearing rap in French strikes some Americans as inherently fancified, the language's felicitous rhymes make for some dazzling wordplay."[7]

As it did in America, rap provided young people throughout Europe with a voice to talk about controversial subjects in their communities and in their countries. In Hamburg, Germany, a young rapper named J created a stir. His raps criticized the government of the new, unified Germany, and commented on the re-emergence of racist and anti-Semitic violence:

> *Someone opened up the cage and out comes Germany again,*
> *the beast no one ever tamed.*[8]

J readily admitted the impact that Chuck D and Public Enemy have had upon his work.

Beyond influencing youth to comment on politics, rap has also inspired entire nations. As Polish communism fell in 1990, a Warsaw radio station adopted N.W.A.'s "F—— tha Police," as its theme song.

ASIATIC DISCIPLES When Run-D.M.C. toured Japan in the 1980s, they were surprised (but pleased) to find Japanese b-boys, dressed in unlaced sneakers, glasses, and warm-ups, following their every movement. Rap caught on in Japan and spread like wildfire throughout Asia. In Japan, the group Zingi made militant raps in the street language of Tokyo. Kayto Ochi, a rapper from Southeast Asia, dropped rhymes that bragged as much as those of L.L. Cool J:

> *They call me Kayto*
> *a hard rappin' Asian.*
> *I'll make you sweat no matter your persuasion,*
> *Cos bustin' rhymes is my occupation, yo!*[9]

Rapper Baba Sehgal, who sampled Vanilla Ice records, became a major star in India.

RETURN TO THE MOTHERLAND Rap has experienced an especially enthusiastic homecoming on the continent to which it traces its roots. It is tremendously popular with youth across Africa. When a young African meets an African-American visitor, one of his first questions is likely to be "Do you know L.L. Cool J?" or "Have you been to Chuck D's house?" Youth often ask first-time African-Americans visitors to the continent, even the more mature and conservative looking, if they know how to rap. If the answer is negative, the more persistent African chap will argue that "L.L. comes from the same place as you, so why can't you rap?"[10]

Audio tapes of American rap radio programs are hot items that fetch high prices on the black market. The dream of any young African rap fan is to become pen pals with an American youth who can supply cassette copies of the latest hip-hop hits.

In North Africa, the Moroccan group Aisha Kandisha's Jarring Effects (AKJE) took rap and hip-hop into new realms. AKJE started out playing *jajouka*, the traditional spiritual and dance music named for a remote region in the country's northern mountains. Once the band heard American rap, they incorporated elements of it into their centuries-old sound. Music journalist Neil Strauss described their first album, *El Buya*, as "a collision between a busload of visiting hip-hop DJs and a passing band of master musicians of Jajouka."[11] The group Ahlam, also from Morocco, featured on their first album American keyboardist Bernie Worrell, who played with funk king George

Clinton and former Last Poet Umar Bin Hassan. At Ahlam shows, fans whipped themselves into dance frenzies that combined break-dancing with traditional Moroccan belly dancing as they listened to the band's Arabic hip-hop.

In Liberia, the West African country founded by freed American slaves in 1821, young rappers talked about the civil war that destroyed their country in the early 1990s. In Somalia, rap tunes blared throughout the city of Mogadishu as the United States and United Nations peacekeeping forces exchanged posts in 1993.

The South African rap group Prophets of the City dressed like American rappers. But once they opened their mouths, their raps were strictly about growing up in the black townships of their troubled nation. Zimbabwe Legit, made up of the Ndlovu brothers Dumi and Akim, rapped in English and their tribal language, Ndbele. Their first U.S. album was produced by rap group Black Sheep, members of Queen Latifah's Flavor Unit Posse. The crisscrossing of African and African-American music and languages showed that rap had indeed come a long way in order to return home.

Epilogue:
Young Lions
Return.
"The setting was different, but the culture was the same." So said the South African journalist Mondli Makhanya of the Souls of Mischief at the beginning of this book. Perhaps the same can be said of all rap. While rap has grown and spread beyond anyone's wildest imagination, it has also remained firmly rooted in the African and African-American cultures that produced it. This cooperation between old and new, change and tradition, gives rap its pulse — and promises it a long future.

This point wasn't lost on the Souls of Mischief. Learning of Makhanya's remark, A-Plus said: "The way your man from Soweto felt vibing with us, although he's from thousands of miles away, proves that there is a powerful energy in hip-hop."

"What he vibed on was our realness," added Tajai. "Hip-hop is about staying true to who you are. We're the same people everywhere. There are common elements in all black folks — and in all human beings — that go back to the beginning of time."

Perhaps one of those "common elements" that rap responds to is the need not only to communicate, but to do so creatively. As Tajai put it: "Rap is straight talk. It's that soul within us."

Rap's "soul" is an emotion that people throughout the world can celebrate. "How do you think kids in Japan can get into Boogie Down Productions?" Tajai asked. "You don't always have to know the language, you just have to know how to feel."

And in the end, maybe that's the meaning of the story of rap.

Notes

PROLOGUE
1. Def Jef, "Dropping Rhymes on Drums," *Just a Poet with Soul*, Delicious Vinyl Records, 1989.
2. Hieroglyphics sampler, Jive Records, 1992.
3. Casual, "Let Em Know," Jive Records, 1993.
4. Souls of Mischief, "That's When Ya Lost," Jive Records, 1993.

CHAPTER ONE
1. Wolfgang Bender, "The Griot Style," *Sweet Mothers* (Chicago: University of Chicago Press, 1991), pp. 17–18.
2. *Ibid.*

CHAPTER TWO
1. Gil Scott-Heron, "The Revolution Will Not be Televised," BMG Music, 1974.
2. W.E.B. Du Bois, "Of the Faith of the Fathers," *The Souls of Black Folk* (New York: Penguin Books, 1989), p. 155.
3. C. L. Franklin, "The Prodigal Son," in Goss and Barnes, eds., *Talk that Talk* (New York: Simon & Schuster, 1989), p. 193.
4. Nikki Giovanni, "Ego Tripping," *Recreation* (Detroit: Broadside Press, 1970).
5. Gil Scott-Heron, liner notes, *Free Will*, Flying Dutchman Records, 1972.
6. James Brown, "Say It Loud: I'm Black and I'm Proud," *Star Time*, Columbia Records, 1992.
7. Carl Gayle, "Long Time I No Deejay Inna Dance," *Reggae International* (Munich, Germany: Rogner & Bernhard GMBH & Co. Verlages KG, 1982), p. 111.
8. Linton Kwesi Johnson, "De Eagle & De Bear," *Making History*, Mango Records, 1984.
9. Christian "Chako" Habekost, "Rapso, Riddim Poetry from Trinidad/Tobago," *The Beat*, Vol. 12 #2, 1993, pp. 42–44.
10. Ron Sakolsky, "Brother Resistance: The Voice of the People," *The Beat*, Vol. 12 #2, 1993, pp. 43, 71.
11. William Harris, "A Trinidad Playwright Awash in Words," *The New York Times*, May 9, 1993, Sec. H, p. 1, 21.

CHAPTER THREE 1. Sugar Hill Gang, "Rapper's Delight," Sugar Hill Records, 1979.
2. Hieroglyphics interview, April 22, 1993.
3. Kurtis Blow, "The Breaks," Mercury Records, 1980.
4. Blondie, "Rapture," Chrysalis Records, 1980.

CHAPTER FOUR 1. Grandmaster Flash and the Furious Five, "The Message," Sugar Hill Records, 1982.
2. Will Smith interview, New York and Los Angeles, November 1991.
3. Run-D.M.C., "It's Like That," *Run-DMC*, Profile Records, 1984.
4. Run-D.M.C., "Peter Piper," *Run-DMC*, Profile Records, 1984.
5. L.L. Cool J, "I Can't Live Without My Radio," *Radio*, Def Jam Records, 1985.
6. L.L. Cool J, "Rock the Bells," *Bigger and Deffer*, Def Jam Records, 1987.
7. Jenette Beckman and Bill Adler, *Rap* (New York: St. Martin's Press, 1991), p. 63.
8. Greg Tate, "The Devil Made 'Em Do It: Public Enemy," *Flyboy in the Buttermilk* (New York: Simon & Schuster, 1992), p. 125.
9. Easy Mo Bee interview, New York City, December 1992.
10. Public Enemy, "Fight the Power," *Fear of a Black Planet*, CBS Records, 1989.
11. Public Enemy, "Welcome to the Terror Dome," *Fear of a Black Planet*, CBS Records, 1989.
12. *Ibid.*
13. Boogie Down Productions, "House Niggas," Jive Records, 1991.
14. KRS-One, press biography, Jive Records, 1991.
15. Boogie Down Productions, "You Must Learn," *Ghetto Music: The Blueprint of Hip-Hop*, Jive Records, 1989.
16. KRS-One interview, Newark, N.J., April 1992.
17. Ice Cube, "The Funeral," *Death Certificate*, Priority Records, 1991.
18. Ice Cube, *The Predator*, Profile Records, 1992.
19. Easy Mo Bee interview, op. cit.
20. DJ Jazzy Jeff and the Fresh Prince, "Nightmare on My Street," *And in This Corner . . .* Jive Records, 1989.
21. Will Smith interview, *op. cit.*
22. Ibid.

23. Young MC, "I Come Off," *Stone Cold Rhymin'*, Delicious Vinyl, 1989.

24. Roxanne Shanté, press biography, Cold Chillin' Records, 1987.

25. Roxanne Shanté, "Have a Nice Day," Cold Chillin' Records, 1987.

26. Queen Latifah, "Come Into My House," *All Hail the Queen*, Tommy Boy Records, 1989.

27. Yo Yo, "Make Way for the Motherload," *Make Way for the Motherload*, East/West Records, 1991.

28. Havelock Nelson and Michael A. Gonzales, "Vanilla Ice," *Bring on the Noise* (New York: Harmony Books, 1991), pp. 268–270.

29. The Beastie Boys, "Hold It Now—Hit It!" *License to Ill*, Def Jam Records, 1986.

30. 3rd Bass, "Product of the Environment," *The Cactus Album*, Def Jam Records, 1990.

31. 3rd Bass, "Pop Goes the Weasel," *Derelicts of Dialect*, Def Jam, 1991.

32. Super Cat interview, New York City, July 1992.

33. Shabba Ranks, "Roots and Culture," *The Best of Dancehall, Vol 2.*, Profile Records, 1990.

34. A Tribe Called Quest, "Excursion," *The Low End Theory*, Jive Records, 1992.

35. Arrested Development, "Tennessee," *3 Years, 5 Months and 2 Days in the Life of . . .* , Chrysalis Records, 1992.

36. *DJ Times*, April 1992

37. Meg Cox, "Rap Music Is Taking a Positive Turn and Winning Fans," *The Wall Street Journal*, October 8, 1992, Sec. A, p. 1.

38. Guru, "Intro," *Jazzmatazz*, Chrysalis, 1993.

CHAPTER FIVE 1. Paris, "Break the Grip of Shame," *The Devil Made Me Do It*, Tommy Boy Records, 1990.

2. Easy Mo Bee interview, *op. cit.*

3. Souls of Mischief interview. *op. cit.*

4. Digital Underground, "No Nose Job," *Sons of the P*, Tommy Boy Records, 1992.

5. Kierna Mayo, "When Russell Talks," *The Source*, February 1993, pp. 50–51.

6. Jefferson Morley, "Rap Music as American History," in Lawrence A. Stanley, ed., *Rap The Lyrics* (New York: Penguin Books, 1992), Introduction.

7. Henry Louis Gates, "2 Live Crew, Decoded," *The New York Times*, June 19, 1990, Sec. A, p. 23.
8. Ice T, "Freedom of Speech," *Freedom of Speech*, Warner Brothers, 1989.
9. James Baldwin, "Fifth Avenue, Uptown," *Nobody Knows My Name*, (New York: Vintage International Edition, 1993) pp. 65–66.
10. Super Cat interview, *op. cit.*
11. Jon Pareles, "The Disappearance of Ice T's 'Cop Killer,'" *The New York Times*, July 30, 1993, Sec. C, p. 13.
12. Cornell West, "Introduction," *Race Matters* (Boston: Beacon Press, 1993), pp. 4–5.
13. Paris interviews, New York and Oakland, March 1991.
14. Public Enemy, "Burn Hollywood Burn," *Fear of a Black Planet*, CBS Records, 1990.
15. Shelia Rule, "Rappers Say the Riots Were No Surprise to Their Listeners," *The New York Times*, May 6, 1992, Sec. C, p. 13.
16. David Mills, "Sister Souljah's Call to Arms," *The Washington Post*, May 13, 1992, Sec B P:1.
17. Greg Tate, *op. cit.*
18. Shelia Rule, *op. cit.*

CHAPTER SIX
1. Digital Underground, "The Humpty Dance," *Sex Packets*, Tommy Boy Records, 1990.
2. Nelson George, *Listen Up, The Lives of Quincy Jones* (New York: Warner Books, 1990), pp. 163–167.
3. Quincy Jones, "Back on the Block," *Back on the Block*, Warner Brothers/Qwest Records, 1989.
4. Shabba Ranks (featuring Maxi Priest), "House Call," *As Raw as Ever*, Epic Records, 1991.
5. The Winans, "It's Time," *Return*, Warner Brothers/Quest Records, 1991.
6. Mike E. interview, 1993.
7. Devlin Donaldson, "Center Stage—Mike E," *Bookstore Journal*, October 1991.
8. Mike E. "Good News for Bad Timez," *Good News for Bad Timez*, Reunion Records, 1993.
9. Robert Townsend interview, New York-Los Angeles, February 1993.

CHAPTER SEVEN 1. Zimbabwe Legit, "To Bead or Not to Bead," *Zimbabwe Legit*, Hollywood Basic Records, 1992.

2. David Sinclair, "Rapping the World," *Billboard*, November 28, 1992, p. 1.

3. William Middleton, "New Jacques City," *Vibe*, Fall 1992, p. 136.

4. Ibid.

5. A. Scott Galloway, "Two New Jazz-Rap Projects," *Rap Sheet*, June 1993.

6. Middleton, *op. cit.*

7. John Rockwell, "Felicitous Rhymes, and Local Roots," *The New York Times*, August 23, 1992, Sec. B, p. 23.

8. Mike Hennessey, Ken Terry, and Paul Verna, "German Rappers Take Aim at Racism," *Billboard*, September 26, 1992, p. 1, 97.

9. David Sinclair, *op. cit.*

10. Dialogue with a youth in Kitwe, Zambia.

11. Neil Strauss, "Morocco's New Edge," *Option*, March/December 1993, p. 64.

A Glossary of Hip-Hop Terms

Back in the day: the early days of rap or one's childhood.
Bite: to copy someone else's rap or style.
Boomin': a good groove; exceptional.
Breakin': verbally abusing someone.
Buggin': behaving irrationally.

Chill: to take it easy.
Clockin': observing a situation.
Crew: a set of close friends.

Def: very positive.
Dope: really cool.
Down: to be in agreement or unified with someone or something.
Droppin' science: communicating truth or cultural integrity in rap
    or regular speech.

Flavor: heart, soul.
Fly: cool, hip, exceptional.
Freestyle: improvisational rap usually done in live settings as a
    result of a challenge.
Fresh: exceptional.
Frontin': putting up a front; being deceptive.

G: a close friend or girlfriend.
Got it going on: having it all together.

Hard: authentic; undiluted.

'Hood: one's neighborhood.
Hype: an extremely good groove or situation.

Ill: unacceptable behavior.
In full effect: an exceptional performance; no holds barred.
In the house: acknowledgment of the presence of peers.

Jam(mie): song.
Joint: the best.
Juice: respect on the streets.

Living large: an affluent lifestyle; success.

Max: to relax.

New jack swing: rhythm and blues of the 1980's and 1990's incorporating rap.

Old school: old style rap like that of Kurtis Blow and Kool Moe Dee.

Peep: preview; an honor bestowed on the cool.
Phat: state of the art.

Raggamiffin: Jamaican dancehall.

Slammin': an unrelenting groove or action.
Sucker MCs: inferior rappers.
Sweatin': pressuring someone.

Tip: serious treatment of a subject.

Wack: uncool or bizarre behavior.
Waxin': to humiliate inferior MCs.

Discography

Arrested Development. *3 Years, 5 Months & 2 Days in the Life of. . . .*
    Chrysalis, 1992.

The Beastie Boys. *License to Ill.* Def Jam, 1986.

Big Daddy Kane. *It's a Big Daddy Thing.* Cold Chillin'/Reprise, 1989.
Boogie Down Productions. *Ghetto Music: The Blueprint of Hip-Hop.*
    Jive Records, 1989.
Brand New Heavies. *Heavy Rhyme Experience*, Vol. 1., Delicious Vinyl, 1992.

Miles Davis. *Doo-Bop.* Warner, 1992.
DJ Jazzy Jeff and the Fresh Prince. *And in This Corner.* Jive Records, 1989.
Def Jef. *A Poet with Soul.* Delicious Vinyl, 1989.
Digable Planets. *Reachin' a New Refutation of Time and Space.* Elektra, 1992.
Digital Underground. *Sons of the P.* Tommy Boy Records, 1992.

Guru. *Jazzamatazz.* Chrysalis, 1993.

Hammer. *Please Hammer Don't Hurt 'Em.* Capitol Records, 1991.

Ice Cube. *AmeriKKKa's Most Wanted.* Priority Records, 1990.
_____.*Death Certificate.* Priority Records, 1991.
Ice T. *Rhyme Pays.* Warner, 1985.
_____.*Freedom of Speech.* Warner, 1989.

KRS-One. *Return of the Bam Boom.* Jive, 1993.

Leaders of the New School. *Leaders of the New School.* Elektra, 1991.
L.L. Cool J. *Mama Said Knock You Out.* Def Jam, 1990.
_____.*Radio.* Def Jam, 1985.

Martin Lawrence. *Talking Sh——t.* East/West, 1993.
Mike E. *Good News for Bad Timez.* Warner, 1992.

Naughty by Nature. *19NaughtyIII.* Tommy Boy, 1993.
NWA. *Straight Outta Compton.* Ruthless, 1988.

Greg Osby. *3-D Lifestyles.* Blue Note, 1993.

Paris. *The Devil Made Me Do It.* Tommy Boy, 1989.
Public Enemy. *It Takes a Nation of a Million to Hold Us Back.*
    Def Jam, 1988.
_____.*Fear of a Black Planet.* Def Jam, 1990.

Queen Latifah. *All Hail the Queen.* Tommy Boy, 1989.

Run-D.M.C. *Run-D.M.C. Down with the King.* Profile, 1993.

Salt N' Pepa. *Hot, Cool & Vicious.* Next Plateau Records, 1986.
Shabba Ranks. *As Raw as Ever.* Epic, 1992.
Roxanne Shanté. *Bad Sister.* Cold Chillin', 1989.
MC Solaar. *Qui Seme Le Vent Repolte Le Tempo.* Polydor, 1991.
Super Cat. *Don Dada.* Columbia, 1992.

3rd Bass. *The Cactus Album.* Def Jam, 1989.
Too Short. *Life Is Too Short.* Dangerous Music, 1988.
A Tribe Called Quest. *Low End Theory.* Jive Records, 1992.
_____.*People's Instinctive Travels and the Paths of Rhythm*,
    1990.

Young MC. *Stone Cold Rhymin'.* Delicious Vinyl, 1989.
Yo Yo. *Make Way for the Motherlode.* East/West Records, 1991.

Further Reading

ABOUT RAP   Adler, Bill and Jenette Beckman. *Rap.* New York: St. Martin's Press, 1991.

Campbell, Luther and John R. Miller. *As Nasty as They Wanna Be.* Fort Lee, NJ: Barricade Books, 1992.

George, Nelson. *Stop the Violence.* New York: National Urban League and Pantheon Books, 1990.

Greenberg, Keith. *Rap.* Minneapolis: Lerner, 1990.

McCoy, Judy. *Rap Music in the 1980s: A Reference Guide.* Metuchen, NJ: Scarecrow Press, 1992.

Nelson, Havelock and Michael Gonzales. *Bring the Noise: A Guide to Rap and Hip-Hop.* New York: Harmony Books, 1991.

Spady, James G. and Joseph D. Eure. *Nation Conscious Rap.* New York: PC International, 1991.

Stanley, Lawrence A. and Jefferson Morely. *Rap: The Lyrics.* New York: Penguin Books, 1992.

Tate, Greg. *Flyboy in the Buttermilk.* New York: Simon and Schuster, 1992.

Toop, David. *Rap Attack 2: African Rap to Global Hip-Hop.* London: Serpent's Tail, 1992.

ABOUT AFRICAN-AMERICAN CULTURE RELATED TO RAP

Baldwin, James. *Nobody Knows My Name.* New York: Vintage International, 1993.

Bender, Wolfgang. *Sweet Mother Tongue: Modern African Music.* Chicago: University of Chicago Press, 1991.

Brown, Elaine. *A Taste of Power: A Black Woman's Story.* New York: Pantheon, 1992.

Brown, James and Bruce Tucker. *James Brown: Godfather of Soul.* New York: Thunders Mouth Press, 1990.

Du Bois, W.E.B. *The Souls of Black Folk.* New York: Penguin Books, 1989.

Genovese, Eugene D. *Roll, Jordan Roll: The World the Slaves Made.* New York: Vintage, 1976.

George, Nelson. *Listen Up: The Lives of Quincy Jones.* New York: Warner Books, 1990.

Giovanni, Nikki. *Recreation.* Detroit: Broadside Press, 1970.

Gross, Linda and Marian E. Barnes, eds. *Talk that Talk: An Anthology of African-American Storytelling.* New York: Simon & Schuster, 1989.

Leifer, Neil and Thomas Hauser. *Muhammad Ali: Memories.* New York: Rizzoli, 1992.

Murray, Albert. *Stomping the Blues.* New York: Vintage Books, 1982.

West, Cornell. *Race Matters.* Boston: Beacon Press, 1993.

X, Malcolm and Alex Haley. *The Autobiography of Malcolm X.* New York: Grove, 1965.

Index

Italicized page numbers refer to photo inserts 1 and 2.

Aerosmith, 57
"Afro Emblems" (Woodruff), *1–8*
Ahlam, 110–111
Aisha Kandisha's Jarring Effects (AKJE), 110
Ali, Muhammad (Cassius Clay), 33–34
Alternative rap, 76–78
Angelou, Maya, 68
Apache, 70
A-Plus, 11–12, 113
Armstrong, Louis, 29
Arrested Development, *2–6*, 17, 77
Attila the Hun, 40

Backbeat, 38
Baldwin, James, 86–87
Bambaataa, Afrika, *1–7*, 49–50, 107
Banton, Buju, 76
B-boys, *2–2*, 55–58
Beastie Boys, 73, 74
Bender, Wolfgang, 19
Benson, George, 98
Big Youth, 45

Black church, 22–23, 29
Black Power movement, 35, 38
BlackSheep, 70, 111
Blondie, 50, 102
Blow, Kurtis, 48, 55, 63
Blues, 28–29, 68
Body Count, 64, 87
Boogie Down Productions (BDP), 60–61
Boyz N the Hood, 64
Brand Nubian, 94
Broadside Press, 35
Brooks, Gwendolyn, 68
Brother Resistance, 41
Brown, H. "Rap," 35
Brown, James, *1–7*, 28, 37–38, 92
Brown, Shirley, 68, 69
Byrd, Donald, *2–7*

Call and response, 22, 23, 29, 37–38, 69
Calloway, Cab, 29
Calypsonians, 40, 41
Calypso tent competitions, 40
Campbell, Luther, 72, 85, 90
Campbell, Tevin, 98
Carmichael, Stokely, 35

Carson, Johnny, 102
Carter, Ron, 77
Casual, 9–11, 46–47
Chaka Khan, 98
Chitlin' circuit, 28, 32, 46, 85
Christianity, 22
Chuck D (Carlton Ridenhour), *2–2*, 19, 23, 55, 58–59, 70, 91, 109
Clinton, Bill, 91–92
Clinton, George, *1–7*, 63, 110–111
Comedians, 30–32, 46, 85
"Cop Killer," 64, 87–89
Cypress Hill, 103

Daddy Freddy, 75
Daddy Grace, 33
Dancehall, 39, 56, 75–76
Davis, Miles, 29, 98
Davis, Stephen, 39
Deejays, 30, 39, 45–48
Del Tha Funkee Homosapien, 9
Digable Planets, *2–6*, 77
Digital Underground, *2–4*, 82, 96
Dillinger, 45

Disco, 45
Double meanings, 23
Dozens, 31–32
Du Bois, W.E.B., *1–5*, 32, 62
Dumas, Henry, *1–8*

Easy Mo Bee, 65, 81–82
"Ego Tripping (There May Be a Reason Why)" (Giovanni), 35–36
Emancipation Proclamation, 27

Fab 5 Freddy, 50, 102, 107
Fat Boys, 58
Father Divine, 33
Feles for Sale (Searles), *1–8*
Female rappers, *2–5*, 68–71
Folktales, 23–24
Foxx, Redd, 30, 85
Franklin, Aretha, 32
Franklin, C. L., 32–33, 92
Freestyle Fellowship, 77
Fresh Prince (Will Smith), *2–3*, 55, 56, 66–67

Gang Starr, 77, 78
Gangster rappers, 63–65
Garvey, Marcus, 49
Gates, Henry Louis, Jr., 84–85
Gershwin, George, 71

Geto Boys, 55–56, 63
Gettin' Religion (Motley,) *1–3*
Ghettoese, 64
Gillespie, Dizzy, 29, 98
Giovanni, Nikki, 35–36, 68
Gore, Tipper, 85, 86
Gospel music, 28, 99–100
Grandmaster Flash and the Furious Five, 50, 54, 55
Great Migration, *1–2*, 27–28
Green, Grant, 77
Griots, 18–19, 24, 37, 56, 78
Guru, *2–7*

Habekost, Chako, 41
Hall, Arsenio, 102
Hammer, 37, 72, 74, 93, 101
Handy, W. C., 28
Hank, Big Bank, 48
Harris, Eddie, 77
Harry, Debbie, 50
Hayden, Robert, *1–3*
Heavy D. (Dwight Myers), 75
Herc, DJ Kool, 45–46
Hieroglyphics, 9
Hollywood, DJ, 45
Human Education Against Lies (HEAL), 61

Humpty Hump, *2–4*, 82–83

Ice Cube, *2–3*, 23, 63–65, 88, 91, 100, 103
Ice-T (Tracy Morrow), *2–3*, 19, 35, 55, 63–64, 86–89, 94, 98, 100, 103
I-Roy, 45
Islam, 33, 34

J, 109
Jackson, Jesse, 32, 102
Jackson, Michael, 97
Jackson, Millie, 68, 69
Jamaicans, 38–40, 45, 75, 98–99
James, Rick, 63, 93
Jazz, *1–3*, *2–7*, 29–30, 77
Jazz Crusaders, 77
Jazzy Jeff, DJ, 66
JBs, 37
Jimmy Castor Bunch, 45
Jive, 30
Johnson, Linton Kwesi, 40
Jones, Philly Jo, 29
Jones, Quincy, 67, 97–98
Jordan, Louis, 29

Kane, Big Daddy, 81, 98
Kid 'N Play, 101, 103
King, Martin Luther, Jr., 32, 35
Kool and the Gang, 45
Kool Moe Dee, 98

Kora, 19
KRS-One (Kris Parker), 2–7, 35, 56, 60–62, 70

LaRock, Scott, 60–61
Last Poets, The, 35
Latifah, Queen (Dana Owens), 2–5, 17, 35, 68–70, 81
Lawrence, Jacob, 1–2
Lee, Don L. (Haki Madhubuti), 35, 36
Lee, Spike, 27
Leno, Jay, 102
Lincoln, Abraham, 27
Literacy, 24, 61
L.L. Cool J, 2–1, 32, 34, 55, 57–58, 92, 97, 109
Lord Kitchener, 40
Louis, Joe, 33
Lyte, MC, 68

Mabley, Jackie "Moms," 30, 31
Mad Cobra, 75
Malcolm X, 1–6, 32, 49
Malkhanya, Mondli, 9, 13
Markham, Pigmeat, 30, 31
Markie, Biz, 32, 93–94
Marsalis, Branford, 2–7
Mason, Barbara, 68
Matura, Mustapha, 41–42
Mayfield, Curtis, 45
McDaniels, Darryl (D.M.C.), 56

MCs, 46–48
Melle Mel, 55, 98
Middle Passage, 20–21
Mighty Sparrow, 40
Migration of the Negro, The (Lawrence), 1–2
Mike E., 100–101
Mizell, Jason (Jam Master Jay), 56
Monie Love, 68
Moore, Rudy Ray, 30–31, 85
Morton, Jelly Roll, 28
Motley, Archibald, 1–3
Mutaburuka, 39

National Urban League, 61
Native Americans, 20
Naughty by Nature, 2–5, 19, 70, 94, 103
Nice, Pete, 73–74
Nice and Smooth, 94
North Atlantic Slave Trade, 17–18, 20–21
N.W.A. (Niggas With Attitude), 64, 90, 91

Ochi, Kayto, 109
O'Connor, Sinead, 1–7
Opio, 11, 12
Oration, 18
Osby, Greg, 78
Owens, Jesse, 33

Page, Lawanda, 30

Parents Music Resource Center (PMRC), 85–86
Paris, 35, 80, 89–90
Parker, Charlie "Yardbird," 29
Parker, Maceo, 37, 38
PG rappers, 55, 66–67
Phesto, 11–12
Picong, 40
Poets, 35–36, 39, 68
Preacher (White), 1–5
Preachers, 1–3, 1–5, 22–24, 32–33, 36
Presley, Elvis, 71, 72
Priest, Maxi, 98–99
Prince Far-I, 45
Prophet Jones, 33
Prophets of the City, 111
Pryor, Richard, 31
Public Enemy, 1–7, 2–2, 17, 55, 58–59, 90, 91, 93, 100, 101, 109
Punk rockers, 50

Rakim, 55
Ranks, Shabba, 75–76, 98–99
Rapso, 41
Reconstruction Era, 27
Reggae, 75–76
Ren, MC (Lorenzo Patterson), 91
Rich, Richie, 73
Riley, Teddy, 99–100
Roach, Max, 29
Robinson, Jackie, 33

127

Robinson, Sylvia, 48
Rollins, Sonny, 77
Run-D.M.C., *2–2*, 56–58, 97, 109

Salt-N'-Pepa, 68, 70–71, 92
Sampling, 28, 92–94
Sanchez, Sonia, 35, 68
Scott-Heron, Gil, 26, 36–37, 39
Scratching, 47
Searles, Charles, *1–8*
Sehgal, Baba, 110
Selectors, 39
Serch, MC, *2–6*, 73
Shadow, 40
Shanté, Roxanne (Lolita Gooden), 68–70
Sharecropping, 27
Shinehead, 75
Simmons, Joseph (Run), 56
Simmons, Russell, 83
Simon, Peter, 39
Singleton, John, 64
Slavery, *1–2*, 18, 20–24, 27
Sly Stone, 45
Smith, Bessie, *1–4*, 28
Smith, Michael, 39

Solaar, MC, 108
Souljah, Sister (Lisa Williamson), 91–92
Souls of Black Folk, The (Du Bois), *1–5*
Souls of Mischief, *2–8*, 9–12, 113
Spirituals, 24, 28
Stop the Violence project, 61
Sugar Hill Gang, 44, 47–48, 63, 92–93
Supercat, 75, 88

Tajai, 11, 82, 113
3rd Bass, *2–6*, 72–74
Toasting, *1–7*, 39, 56
Too Short, 63, 89, 94
Townsend, Robert, 103
Tribe Called Quest, A, 77
Trinidadians, 38, 40–42
Troupe, Quincy, *1–6*
Tubman, Harriet, 24
2 Live Crew, 72, 84–85, 89, 90
2 Pac, 103

Underground Railroad, 24
U-Roy, *1–7*, 45

UTFO, 68

Vanilla Ice (Robbie Van Winkle), 72–74

Walker, Margaret, 68
Waller, Thomas "Fats," 29
War, 94
Waring, Laura, *1–5*
Wesley, Fred, 37, 38
White, Charles, *1–5*
White, Slappy, 30
White rappers, *2–6*, 71–74
Winans, The, 99, 100
Woodruff, Hale, *1–8*
Worrell, Bernie, 110
Wright, Betty, 68, 69
Writers, 35, 68

Young, Lester "Prez," 29
Young Black Teenagers, 72
Young M.C. (Marvin Young), 55, 66, 67
Yo Yo (Yolanda Whitaker), 68, 70, 71

Zimbabwe Legit, *2–7*, 106, 111
Zulu Nation, 49–50